Faith and Human Rights

FACETS

Selected Titles in the Facets Series

Faith and Human Rights

Christianity and the Global
Struggle for Human Dignity

Richard Amesbury
and George M. Newlands

Fortress Press
Minneapolis

FAITH AND HUMAN RIGHTS
Christianity and the Global Struggle for Human Dignity

Cover design: Christy J. P. Barker
Cover image: Buddhist monk releasing birds from small cage, low angle view. Copyright © Angelo Cavalli; Getty Images
Interior design: Christy J. P. Barker

Library of Congress Cataloging-in-Publication data

Amesbury, Richard, 1972–
Faith and human rights : Christianity and the global struggle for human dignity / Richard Amesbury and George M. Newlands.
    p. cm.
  Includes bibliographical references.
  ISBN-13: 978-0-8006-2132-2 (alk. paper)
    1. Civil rights—Religious aspects—Christianity. 2. Human rights—Religious aspects—Christianity. I. Newlands, G. M., 1941– II. Title.
BT738.15.A44 2008
261.7—dc22   2007044250

ISBN 978-0-8006-2132-2

The paper used in this publication meets the minimum requirements for American National Standard for Information Sciences—Permanence of Paper for Printed Library Materials, ANSI Z329.48-1984.

Manufactured in the U.S.A.
11   10   09   08   1   2   3   4   5   6   7   8   9   10

Contents

Introduction

In 1948, the United Nations adopted the Universal Declaration of Human Rights, arguably the most significant moral manifesto to arise out of the horrors of the twentieth century. Sixty years later, the idea of universal human rights remains a critically important but elusive ideal—one that resonates strongly with many people of faith around the world. At the same time, it must be acknowledged that religious people have been among the world's most egregious *violators* of human rights, and that religion remains implicated in—and frequently benefits from—grave injustices. Is the relation between religion and human rights fundamentally adversarial, or do religious traditions harbor moral resources that can be invoked on behalf of human dignity?

The South African human rights activist and Nobel laureate Desmond Tutu recently remarked that "religion is like a knife": it can be used either to kill or to cut bread to feed the hungry.[1] Tutu should know. As a leader in the struggle against apartheid, the Anglican archbishop witnessed firsthand the power of religion both to liberate and to oppress. Recalling the injustices faced by generations of black South Africans, he has said, "I can testify that our own struggle for justice, peace, and equity would have floundered badly had we not been inspired by our Christian faith and assured of the ultimate victory of goodness and truth, compassion and love against their ghastly counterparts."[2] But Tutu's opponents also used religious arguments—for example, arguments appealing to biblical texts about distinctions among peoples—to justify discriminatory, racist policies.[3] Same knife, different purposes.

Like any good analogy, however, this one has its limits. It seems to suggest, for example, that religion is simply a tool that can be employed in the pursuit of independent goals—goals to which religion is itself indifferent.[4] In many cases, to be sure, religion functions in precisely this way—for example, to sanctify otherwise dubious political agendas or to demonize enemies. Thus, we often hear complaints that religion is being "hijacked" by extremists, exploited by politicians, or commodified by charlatans and corporate hucksters. But the conception of religion as politically benign and "morally neutral," an innocent and unwitting puppet in the hands of larger, sometimes sinister forces, ought itself to arouse our critical suspicions.

For one thing, it lets religion off the hook too easily. We can hear it already: "Religion doesn't kill people; people kill people." True, *religion* is not a "thing" or an agent. Indeed, in one important sense, as Wilfred Cantwell Smith pointed out, there are no religions, only religious people. But while religion (in this sense) cannot act on its own, people can be inspired to act on its behalf, and there is often little reason to doubt their sincerity.

Religion can be manipulated, but it is seldom morally neutral. Its ambiguity derives from the fact that the term *religion* names a variety of different phenomena, some of which are hospitable to human dignity and some of which are not. A responsible assessment of religion, or even of any *particular* religion, must acknowledge these tensions and move beyond the sweeping generalizations that unfortunately remain commonplace in popular political commentary. Instead of speaking of "the relation" between "religion" and human rights and then proceeding to render a verdict, either positive or negative, it would be wise to acknowledge that religion takes many forms, and that there is therefore no *single* relationship in which it stands to the idea of human rights.

By "the idea of human rights," we mean generally the claim that

> there is something about each and every human being, simply as a human being, such that certain choices should be made and certain other choices rejected; in particular, certain things ought not to be done to any human being and certain other things ought to be done for every human being.[5]

Put this way, it is clear that the idea of human rights is first and foremost a moral ideal. But it is a moral ideal with political implications, since it entails that the authority of the community and its institutions and leaders is limited vis-à-vis the individual.

Of course, an empirical assessment of religious practice quickly raises questions of a more philosophical and theological nature, particularly for those of us who stand within one or another religious tradition and care about human rights. After all, it is one thing to *acknowledge* religious ambivalence, quite another to *endorse* it. This book explores both sets of questions, giving special (though not exclusive) attention to Christianity and the possibilities for Christian theology and practice. We argue that while faith has much of value to contribute here, the world's religions (including Christianity) will require vigilant hermeneutical reappraisal and critical retrieval if they are to function as genuine partners in the global struggle for human dignity.

But just as it is important to avoid an abstract, essentialized conception of "religion," so too we must be careful not to treat human rights as if they were "moral trump cards," to borrow Michael Ignatieff's phrase. Ignatieff warns against viewing the idea of human rights as a sort of "secular religion" that can be promoted dogmatically and without reference to the social conditions that make talk of rights possible—a temptation he dubs "human rights idolatry."[6] As we shall see, although the idea of human rights makes claims about (and on) all human beings, it is by no means an a priori category with which all human beings are naturally endowed. It has a history—one in which religion played an important role. We argue that these complex relations are best understood as dialectical: the idea of human rights can derive support from, while also standing in judgment over, religion.

Overview

Human rights discourse arises out of lived experience, much of it brutal. To honor that experience and make it central, our book begins not with theory but with a concrete historical example. Chapter 1, "Human Rights and Christian Witness: A Case Study," examines the role played by the Catholic Church in the struggle for human rights in El Salvador. During the 1970s, the Central American nation was governed by a repressive dictatorship supported by the United States. As tensions within Salvadoran society spiraled toward a protracted civil war, the military and national guard responded to pressure from opposition groups and guerrillas by targeting civilians, and thousands were killed by death squads. Amid the fear and chaos, an unlikely advocate of human rights arose in the person of Oscar Romero, Archbishop of San Salvador. Under his remarkable moral leadership, the Catholic Church gained increasing credibility as an honest broker in the conflict. But Romero's work on behalf of human rights brought him into opposition with the political right, and many within the hierarchy of his own church objected to its new public role. Today, Romero is celebrated as a "human rights apostle," a symbol of the liberating potential of prophetic

Christian witness. But faithful witness has its costs, and the history of the church's involvement in the struggle for human rights in Latin America cautions against triumphalism even as it inspires succeeding generations of rights advocates around the world.[7]

Thus far, the meaning of the phrase *human rights* has remained largely implicit. Chapter 2, "What Are Human Rights?" attempts to make this meaning explicit by examining the *concept* of human rights and the history of its development. Although its roots extend back into the Middle Ages and perhaps further, the concept of human rights as we know it today achieved prominence during the Enlightenment, as Europe was undergoing massive social upheavals that threatened the dignity of individual human beings. In the wake of the Holocaust (Shoah) and the Second World War, the late twentieth century saw the recognition of many of these moral aspirations in international law. But as events in recent decades (for example, in Bosnia, Rwanda, and Iraq) have shown all too clearly, this developing human rights regime lacks adequate mechanisms for enforcement. As threats to human dignity change, the language and practice of human rights also will need to adapt, if the promise of human rights is to be realized by more than a fortunate few.

The core idea of human rights—that every human being has dignity and deserves basic respect, irrespective of nationality or social status, gender or sexuality, race or ethnicity, and so on—remains controversial, and its justification continues to be challenged and debated. Indeed, Alasdair MacIntyre has claimed that human rights are fictional creatures, analogous to "witches or unicorns." Chapter 3, "Human Rights and the Problem of Grounding," takes up these philosophical issues by exploring the relationship between our moral reactions and our understanding of what it means to be a person. We argue that the idea of human rights requires an appropriate "ontology of the human," to use a phrase coined by the philosopher Charles Taylor—that is, an account of what it is about human beings such that they merit respect. According to the view for which we argue, the idea of human rights is grounded in *human* dignity, rather than, say, divine commands or natural laws. However, such justifications can take religious forms, insofar as human dignity is understood through the lens of religious faith.

Some contemporary theorists accept the idea of human rights but deny that it can be given a religious justification. After all, they point out, human rights are universal in scope, claiming to encompass all human beings, whereas religion is by nature particular, and not all human beings share a common faith. Louis Henkin has put forward an especially strong version of this objection, to which we respond in chapter 4, "Universal Human Rights and Religious Particularity." We argue that the validity of the idea of human rights does not depend upon universal consensus and can be affirmed from within a nonuniversal context of justification. According to this account, there is no contradiction in principle between the universality of human rights and the particularity of a determinate religious ground. Of course, since the implementation in practice of human rights requires a hospitable social environment, widespread consensus–agreement across religions and cultures–is nevertheless highly desirable. Consequently, we contend, people who care about human rights should welcome efforts by members of traditions other than their own to ground such rights in the distinctive resources available there. It may be hoped that, given a plurality of *particular* contexts of justification, both religious and nonreligious, individuals in different traditions and cultures will be able to affirm one another's dignity and rights as human beings. We briefly examine recent efforts of this kind within Buddhism, Judaism, and Islam. The next two chapters address Christianity in somewhat greater detail.

Christianity's history with respect to human rights is complex and often ambiguous, its contributions inspiring and deeply depressing by turns. Chapter 5, "Christianity and Human Rights: A Historical Perspective," attempts to chart some of these developments, highlighting ways in which Christians have both contributed to and impeded the struggle for human dignity. It is, of course, impossible to do justice to this complexity in the space allotted, and much that deserves attention must unfortunately be left out of our account. We do not doubt that the same story can be told in indefinitely many other ways, or that our version will strike some readers as unnecessarily critical and others as overly sanguine. We intend it only as an introduction. Moreover, it is important to remember that history is always developing; we have not yet reached "the end of history," as philosophers and millenarians have sometimes prematurely supposed. At the moment, in fact, Christianity is undergoing a historic demographic shift from the northern hemisphere to the global south—a move likely to have enormous and perhaps unanticipated implications for its relations with the idea of human rights. One conclusion of our survey, however, is that repentance may be a necessary first step in the process of critical hermeneutical retrieval.

Perhaps the most distinctive theological claim of Christianity—though variously understood and interpreted—is that in Christ, God became flesh and was consequently susceptible to torture and execution. Yet for Christians, love, not victimization, is the final word. Chapter 6, "Toward a Theology of Human Rights," examines the implications of these christological claims not only for a Christian conception of God but also for a theological account of what it means to be human. To the extent that Christology entails a universal conception of human dignity and illuminates the self-dispossessing nature of God's love as a model for human relationships, it can, we suggest, be *for* human rights.

In concluding, we believe that it is appropriate to call attention back to the practical struggle for human dignity, a struggle to which the theoretical concerns addressed earlier in the book are critically important, but in which they are far from sufficient. The postscript offers some suggestions on how, in partnership with others, a reader might contribute to the creation of a "human rights culture."

This book is the product of collaboration between a moral philosopher (Amesbury) and a theologian (Newlands). This introduction and chapters 1 through 4 are by Amesbury; chapters 5 and 6 are by Newlands; we cowrote the postscript. Since (we think) each of our perspectives complements the other, our hope is that the product of this dialogue across disciplinary lines is greater than the sum of its parts.

Acknowledgments

This project benefits as well from the insightful contributions of many conversation partners. Amesbury would like to thank the following friends and colleagues for helpful comments on earlier portions of the manuscript: Abdullahi Ahmed An-Na'im, J. Dean Brackley, S.J., Drew Smith, and Sumner Twiss. He is grateful as well to Marcia Hernández and Andrew Kirschman, S.J., for their hospitality at the University of Central America in San Salvador in March 2007. Travel to El Salvador was made possible by a grant from Valdosta State University; a grant from the Wabash Center for Teaching and Learning in Theology and Religion helped fund research on chapters 2 and 4. Amesbury also thanks Wesley Theological Seminary for its hospitality during the summer of 2006. Newlands acknowledges the support of critical and intelligent friends, including Keith Ewing, David Fergusson, Duncan Forrester, David Jasper, Paul Middleton, Paul Nimmo, Mona Siddiqui, and Allen Smith.

We also would like to thank Michael West and Susan Johnson of Fortress Press for their support of this project.

An earlier version of chapter 4 was published as "Universal Human Rights and Religious Particularity" in *The God of Love and Human Dignity*, ed. Paul Middleton (London: T&T Clark, 2007), 65–84. It is reprinted here with the kind permission of Continuum International Publishing. Chapters 5 and 6 are adapted from George Newlands, *Christ and Human Rights* (Aldershot, UK: Ashgate, 2006). That material is reprinted with the kind permission of Ashgate Publishing.

1

Human Rights and Christian Witness: A Case Study

Bodies of *campesinos* had been piling up in the countryside all week. In San Salvador, the national university had been besieged by the military, and the cathedral was occupied by demonstrators. But on Sunday morning, March 23, 1980, people gathered for Mass in the Sacred Heart Basilica. It was one of the few places where it was still possible to assemble, though even worship was risky: after Mass two weeks earlier, workers cleaning the church had discovered a suitcase bomb containing seventy-two sticks of dynamite, which had failed to detonate. Rising to deliver the homily, Archbishop Oscar Romero condemned the escalating violence and named the week's victims. Described by *Time* magazine as "a small, benign-looking man with spectacles and graying hair,"[1] Romero appealed directly to the Salvadoran army, the national guard, and the police:

Brothers: you are part of our own people. You kill your own *campesino* brothers and sisters. And before an order to kill given by a man, the law of God ought to prevail, which says, "Thou shalt not kill!" No soldier is obliged to obey an order contrary to the law of God. No one has to comply with an immoral law. . . . The church, defender of the rights of God, of the law of God, of human dignity, of the person, cannot remain silent in the face of such an abomination.[2]

The church's radio station was back on the air after its transmitter had been destroyed by a bomb in February, and Romero's voice, rising with emotion as—to thunderous applause—he addressed the government, could be heard around the country:[3] "In the name of God, and in the name of this suffering people whose laments rise to heaven each day more tumultuous, I implore you, I beg you, in God's name I order you: Stop the repression!"[4]

Romero's commitment to human rights and his religious faith were closely intertwined, each nourishing the other. As he saw it, authentic liberation is rooted in faith, and authentic faith demands attention to human rights. "There can be quick liberations," he cautioned, "but only people of faith are going to bring about definitive, solid liberations."[5] Concluding his homily, he remarked, "The church preaches its liberation just as we have studied it today in the Holy Bible—a liberation that includes above all respect for the dignity of the person . . . and from God alone derives its hope and its force."[6]

As Romero knew all too well, however, "people of faith" have been among the world's most egregious violators of human dignity, and religion has frequently been used to legitimate brutal regimes, demonize enemies, and excuse atrocities. Some within Romero's own church objected to his vigorous advocacy of human rights, which they regarded as the dilution of religion by politics (a politics to which they usually objected), whereas many advocates of human rights have tended to view religion as part of the problem rather than part of its solution. This chapter explores these ambiguities in light of the Salvadoran experience. Later chapters will introduce additional considerations of a more philosophical and theological nature, but at the outset, it will be helpful to focus our attention on a concrete example, one that (as we shall see) defies traditional platitudes and frustrates facile armchair theorizing.

The Salvadoran Context

Named in honor of the Savior of the world, El Salvador is squeezed against the Pacific by

Guatemala and Honduras. A land of immense natural beauty, with verdant vistas framed by soaring volcanic peaks, it is the smallest country in Central America and the only one that does not border on the Caribbean. The population at present is approaching seven million, of which the vast majority is either mestizo or indigenous and approximately 9 percent is white. Roman Catholics continue to constitute a majority, but in recent years, the number of Protestant evangelicals (most of them Pentecostals) has been increasing, as is the case in much of Latin America.

By far the most significant social division is between rich and poor. During the colonial period, indigenous communities farmed communal lands known as *ejidos*, but these were abolished after the country achieved independence. In the late nineteenth century, coffee barons consolidated large private estates in a process that left most Salvadorans landless. These *campesinos* toiled as sharecroppers or eked out a meager living as subsistence farmers on rocky hillsides. In 1932, the *campesinos* demanded agrarian reform, but their uprising was brutally suppressed by the Salvadoran military. In the space of a single month, somewhere between ten thousand and thirty thousand people were killed—the exact figures are disputed but staggering in any case—in what came to be called *La Matanza*, the Slaughter. By the time Romero was installed as archbishop in 1977, just fourteen families controlled more than 60 percent of the arable land.[7]

During the 1970s, El Salvador was ruled by a repressive right-wing dictatorship funded by the United States. In 1980, five opposition groups formed the Farabundo Martí National Liberation Front (FMLN), a leftist guerrilla movement named after Agustín Farabundo Martí Rodríguez, the communist leader executed for his role in organizing indigenous *campesinos* during *La Matanza*. The government responded by increasing its repression in an attempt to cut off support for the opposition. By 1981, the conflict between the military and the guerrillas had escalated into a civil war, in which thousands of civilians, particularly in rural areas, were targeted by paramilitary death squads.[8] The brutality of this campaign of extrajudicial killings and "disappearances" is hard to overstate:

> To demoralize and terrify civilians into submission, the military and their accomplices not only killed but mutilated: skinning alive, slitting throats, beheading people, tearing unborn children from their mothers' wombs. Bodies were left in village squares for the

buzzards; no villager would dare touch them
lest they be accused of subversion.[9]

By the end of the civil war in 1992, out of a
total population of around 5 million, approximately 75,000 people had been killed.

Oscar Romero

Oscar Arnulfo Romero y Galdámez was born
to a working-class family in Ciudad Barrios
in 1917. Although he apprenticed as a car-
penter (his father thought a trade would serve
him better than formal schooling), he went
on, despite his father's objections, to enter the
seminary as a young man and was ordained
in Rome in 1942. Romero planned to remain
at the Pontifical Gregorian University to pursue a doctorate in theology, but as a result of
World War II, he was forced to return to El
Salvador just after his twenty-sixth birthday.
For over thirty years, he served as a priest in a
variety of capacities, and in 1974, he became
a bishop. Then, in February 1977, he was
named Archbishop of San Salvador.

By his own account a conservative, bookish
cleric with little interest in political matters,
Romero was appointed to serve as archbishop
largely because it was believed that, unlike the
more progressive Bishop Arturo Rivera Damas,
he would not threaten the traditionally cozy

relationship between the church and the Salvadoran elite. But on March 12, 1977—just two and a half weeks after Romero was installed—history took an unexpected turn. That afternoon, Father Rutilio Grande, a Jesuit priest and advocate of land reform who worked with seminarians building Christian "base communities" in the town of Aguilares, about thirty miles north of the capital, was riding in a jeep with an elderly man and a teenage boy, on his way to celebrate Mass in the town of El Paisnal. The jeep was ambushed, and all three were shot dead.

Father Grande and Romero had been friends, and late that same night, Romero celebrated a funeral mass for the three in Aguilares. The Jesuit theologian Jon Sobrino, who was present, recalls that "as Archbishop Romero stood gazing at the mortal remains of Rutilio Grande, the scales fell from his eyes."[10] Sobrino later wrote, "The murder of Rutilio Grande was the occasion of the conversion of Archbishop Romero."[11] Contrary to all expectations (on the part of his supporters as well as those, including Sobrino himself, who had objected to his nomination as archbishop), Romero went from being a cautious, timid priest to being an outspoken prophet—a critic of the military dictatorship and a defender of human rights. "Never again would he be capable of separating God from the poor, or his faith in God from his defense of the poor."[12] According to Sobrino, it was "Rutilio's death that gave Archbishop Romero the strength for new activity."[13] He became an "apostle for human rights" speaking out on behalf of the poor and oppressed.[14]

In a context in which freedom of expression was restricted and civic institutions suppressed, the Catholic Church in El Salvador under Romero's leadership gained increasing credibility as an independent source of moral authority, a beacon of hope amid the rising violence and confusion. People with few other resources turned to the archbishop for help in locating missing loved ones, as well as for their own protection. Romero became, in effect, the voice of the voiceless. As the Salvadoran human rights lawyer Roberto Cuéllar recalls, Romero "knew how to combine the ethics and truth of the Gospel with legal defense and public denunciation." He was "a human rights ombudsman fundamentally inspired by the Beatitudes: give food to the hungry, provide drink to the thirsty, console the brokenhearted, and visit those who are in prison."[15]

Although Romero's defense of the otherwise defenseless endeared him to the people, it brought him into increasing opposition with the far right. But despite death threats from enemies and warnings from friends, Romero refused bodyguards, preferring to share the lot of the people he served. On Monday, March 24—the day after his appeal to the military—he celebrated Mass in the chapel of the hospital where he lived. Referring to the day's scripture reading, he said:

> You have just heard in Christ's gospel that one must not love oneself so much as to avoid getting involved in the risks of life that history requires of us, and that whoever seeks to avoid danger will lose his or her life. By contrast, whoever out of love for God gives oneself to the service of others will live, like the grain of wheat that dies, but only apparently. . . . Only in undoing itself does it produce the harvest.[16]

As he prepared the bread and wine for the sacrament, a single shot rang out in the small chapel. Fragments of the bullet pierced his heart, and he died within minutes.

The Church, the Poor, and Power

The Jesuit human rights scholar John Langan points out that Christianity has had an ambivalent record with respect to human rights:

> In its history, Christianity has both obstructed and contributed to the realization of human rights. A significant aspect of human rights

theories and movements has been their root-
ing in such Christian values as universal love,
the equality of all persons before God, the
freedom of the person in the face of secular
authority, the eternal worth of the individual
person, the sense of a realm of values which
ought to guide action and which are not to be
subordinated to the political collectivity. But
a significant aspect of human rights theories
and movements has been their criticism of
Christian churches and institutions in so far
as they collaborated in and benefited from
the repression of human rights.[17]

Part of the explanation for this ambivalence is to be found in the various societal
arrangements in which churches have historically existed. Traditionally, Langan suggests,
Christianity has stood in four basic relationships to the larger societies in which Christians have found themselves:

1. It has been a persecuted minority, far
from the centers of power, as in ancient Rome
and modern China.

2. It has had the status of an established,
official church, as (historically) in Britain and
Scandinavia.

3. It has enjoyed the legal protections of a
free association in a pluralistic society, as in
the United States.

4. It has been divided against itself in such a way as to endanger public order, as (recently) in Northern Ireland.[18]

Langan notes that, in general (and perhaps in contrast to what one might initially expect), the extent to which the church has stood up for human rights is *inversely proportional* to the extent to which it has wielded official political power. Even in modern times, "the churches, at least where they were in an established and protected position, had developed a profound ambivalence on the topic of human rights. This was a position that put them in tension with the universalistic, egalitarian, and nonviolent elements found in the New Testament."[19] Christianity, it is clear, is no exception to the principle that power corrupts.

Historically, the relation between church and state in Latin America has been of Langan's second type: the institutional church enjoyed the support of—and in turn lent legitimacy to—the ruling elite. But in the 1960s and 1970s, the Catholic Church in Latin America began moving away from this model, toward an increasing solidarity with the poor. The initial impetus behind this shift was the Second Vatican Council (1962–1965), with its emphasis on empowering lay people. But it gathered momentum after the Latin American

Bishops' Conference (CELAM) met in Medellin, Columbia (1968), and again in Puebla, Mexico (1979), where it endorsed what it called the "preferential option for the poor." The precise meaning of this suggestive expression is still debated. Some interpret it as a pastoral priority on the part of the church, whereas others understand it to mean that God too is on the side of the poor and oppressed. But the implications were clear: the church must immerse itself in the struggle for liberation. These themes were championed and further developed by Latin American liberation theologians, who argued that scripture and the demands of faith are best interpreted from the viewpoint of the marginalized.

One practical way of empowering lay people was through the sponsorship of ecclesiastical base communities (CEBs, as they are known by their acronym in Spanish and Portuguese). These groups, which were pioneered in Brazil, were typically made up of anywhere from ten to thirty people, who would gather regularly for prayer, Bible study, and discussion. Because the CEBs emphasized critical thinking, democratic lay leadership, and interpreting and applying scripture in light of the current social context, people who were otherwise disenfranchised were empowered to raise questions, exercise authority, and speak out.

These changes in the church happened to coincide with the emergence of extremely repressive political regimes in Latin America. Daniel Levine and Scott Mainwaring, political scientists who have studied base communities in Latin America, write, "Because normal political channels (parties, unions, neighborhood associations) were closed, church-sponsored groups and activities inadvertently became the only available political outlets in some countries."[20] So even though the initial impetus behind the CEBs was religious rather than overtly political, they became extremely politically important.[21] Romero remarks in his Third Pastoral Letter (1978) that although the function of base communities is to study the Bible, scripture "makes demands" on people which "can awaken political commitment."[22]

But the rise of these liberationist movements and their alliance with existing opposition groups (for example, of *campesinos*, workers, and students) also meant that the church came increasingly to be perceived as a threat to the existing social order, not only by authoritarian governments in Latin America, but also by the government of the United States, which was at the time involved in a Cold War in which Latin American "proxy states" were the pawns. Siding with the poor meant forfeiting the privileges and protections of power. By identifying itself with the people, the Catholic Church in El Salvador had become something not represented in Langan's typology—in effect, a persecuted *majority.*

Mixed Reactions

An allegorical painting by Benjamin Cañas depicts the fallen Romero, surrounded by various figures. Kneeling beside him, tending his body like Mary in a traditional pietà, is a nude woman, who represents the poor. A soldier—one of the men Romero had addressed as "brothers"—looks sorrowfully at the archbishop, over the shoulder of a nun. A prelate in a pointed hat, wearing a ring, rests a hand on Romero's chest, but his gaze is fastened on a stylized crucifix on the wall behind him. He seems to notice neither the lifeless body in front of him nor that his heel is resting on a naked infant, the child of the poor. As suggested by the painting, which hangs in the Archbishop Oscar Romero Center at the Jesuit-run University of Central America in San Salvador, Romero's campaign for human rights met with mixed reactions, even within his own church.

Some critics claimed that the preferential option for the poor conflicted with the universality of the church's salvific mission, and that the church should avoid political entanglements. Romero struggled with these same theological reservations during his own lifetime. As a priest and later a bishop, he valued peace and unity; by taking the side of the poor and oppressed against the elite, liberation theology initially seemed to Romero to be divisive. Eventually, though, he concluded that true peace requires justice, and that passivity is no less political than action, insofar as it helps to maintain the status quo. He wrote:

> The world of the poor teaches us what the nature of Christian love is, a love that certainly seeks peace, but also unmasks false pacifism—the pacifism of resignation and inactivity. . . . The world of the poor teaches us that the sublimity of Christian love ought to be mediated through the overriding necessity of justice for the majority.[23]

The Vatican, for its part, has long had its suspicions about liberation theology and its proponents. Under the leadership of Cardinal Joseph Ratzinger, the Sacred Congregation for the Doctrine of the Faith, the Vatican's doctrinal watchdog group (formerly known as the "Holy Office"), in 1984 published a document entitled "Instruction on Certain Aspects of the 'Theology of Liberation.'" Although it concedes that the widespread desire for liberation among the world's downtrodden attests to an "authentic, if obscure, perception of the dignity of the human person," the instruction charges that some liberation theologians "use, in an insufficiently critical manner, concepts borrowed from various currents of Marxist thought" and contends that "one needs to be on guard against the politicization of existence which, misunderstanding the entire meaning of the Kingdom of God and the transcendence of the person, begins to sacralize politics and betray the religion of the people in favor of the projects of the revolution." The following year, Ratzinger imposed an "obedient silence" on the distinguished Brazilian theologian Leonardo Boff, thereby putting on notice the church's more progressive theologians.[24]

Recently, the Vatican's attention has shifted to the theology of Romero's friend and adviser, Jon Sobrino. On March 14, 2007, two days after the thirtieth anniversary of Rutilio Grande's death, the Vatican released a "Notification" on Sobrino's theology, which it said contained "erroneous or dangerous propositions." In the fourteen-page document, the Congregation for the Doctrine of the Faith asserts that Sobrino fails to give sufficient attention to the divinity of Jesus.[25] The notification was approved by Ratzinger, who had taken the name Benedict XVI after his election to the papacy in 2005.

Other recent critics of liberation theology contend not that it is unorthodox, but that it is irrelevant, a relic of a bygone era. Times have changed, and without the conditions that gave rise to it (authoritarian dictatorships and Marxist revolutions, the Cold War, and so on), it lacks a cogent raison d'être. Some commentators see the future of global Christianity not in a spirit of solidarity with those struggling for sociopolitical liberation and human rights, but in a return to biblical literalism, legalistic personal morality, and hierarchical patterns of ecclesiastical and political authority. In response, Sobrino has written, "The origin, thrust, and direction of the theology of liberation is not in socialism, but in the experience of God in the poor, an experience of grace and exigency. Therefore so long as this experience exists and is conceptualized, there can be a theology of liberation."[26]

Ongoing Challenges

Dragón, a towering sculpture by Salvadoran artist Napoleón Alberto Escoto, depicts a green monster standing over a torn pamphlet labeled *Declaración Universal de los Derechos Humanos* (Universal Declaration of Human Rights). The spines on the dragon's back are made of bullets, and it has trampled the scales of justice beneath its feet. However, the dragon's neck has been cleft by a *cuma*—a curved machete used by *campesinos* in the sugarcane fields—and the fearful creature is in the throes of death. Completed in 1993, the year after peace accords brought an end to El Salvador's civil war, the work highlights both the terror of the past and the possibility of a better future. The monster is still alive, but it has been mortally wounded.

Much has changed for the better since the war ended, but significant challenges remain. Among these is the difficulty of coming to terms with history. A monument in San Salvador's central park, the Parque Cuscatlán, honors the victims of twenty-one years of political repression and civil war. Etched in a black stone wall are the names of thousands of individuals who were murdered or "disappeared." Some are household names—Oscar Romero and Rutilio Grande, among them—but the vast majority are unfamiliar, the names of *campesinos* and workers. They are all but forgotten by history, if not by those who loved them. The wall, which resembles Maya Lin's Vietnam Veterans Memorial in Washington, D.C., is called a Monument to Memory and Truth. Set into a hillside beneath a busy thoroughfare, it serves as a buttress against the forces of forgetfulness and historical revision that threaten to relegate these otherwise anonymous victims to oblivion. Written in red paint at the end of this grim roll call are the words *"Ni perdon ni olvido—exigimos la verdad sobre los desaparecidos"* ("We will neither forgive nor forget—we demand the truth about the disappeared").

But there is also a desire among some Salvadorans to forget the past, even to erase it. In 2007, the nation's ruling party, the Republican Alliance (ARENA), introduced legislation—ultimately unsuccessfully—to grant (posthumously) the nation's highest honor, the title of *Hijo Meritísimo*, to the party's founder, Roberto D'Aubuisson. It was D'Aubuisson, commander of the right-wing death squads, who had given the order to assassinate Romero. D'Aubuisson escaped conviction for any crimes during his lifetime, only to die of throat cancer in 1992. Indeed, the vast majority of human rights abuses committed during the war have gone unpunished, as a result of the General Amnesty Law, passed in 1993.

Violence remains endemic. After years of civil war, trust is low, whereas guns are plentiful. El Salvador's murder rate is among the highest in the world. Much of the violence is perpetrated by gangs known locally as *maras*. The term derives from *marabunta*, the name of an aggressive ant species. Interestingly, the *maras* got their start in the United States, among Salvadoran war refugees and their children. When crackdowns on gang violence in the 1990s led to the deportation of thousands of undocumented immigrant gang members, the *maras* quickly reorganized in Central America, where they have become involved with international drug cartels. Efforts to combat the violence have tended to exacerbate it. Human rights groups have criticized the government of El Salvador for its harsh antigang measures, dubbed the *Mano Dura* (the Iron Fist).

At the root of many of El Salvador's ongoing human rights challenges lies the continuing vast disparity between rich and poor. El Salvador signed on to the Central American Free Trade Agreement (CAFTA) in 2003, but the results of economic growth are unequally distributed. More than 60 percent of rural Salvadorans lack running water in the home, and nearly two-thirds of the total population survive on less than two dollars a day; perhaps half of these endure extreme poverty.[27] Here, as elsewhere in the "developing" world, children still die of diarrhea and other preventable diseases.

The Struggle Continues

Among the poor of El Salvador, to whom he is already *San Romero*, the archbishop's legacy lives on. By midafternoon on the anniversary of his death, a crowd has gathered at the Plaza las Americas, growing larger by the minute. A folk ensemble is performing a song by Salvadoran artist Jorge Palencia, entitled *"El Profeta"* ("The Prophet"). Everyone knows the words, and they join in on the chorus:

> *Podrán matar al profeta*
> *Pero su voz de justicia no,*
> *Y le impondrán el silencio*
> *Pero la historia no callará.*

> They can kill the prophet
> But not his voice of justice,
> And they will command silence
> But history will not keep quiet.

Those assembled erupt into applause as each new delegation of parishioners arrives. Soon the neighborhood is teeming with people, and police close surrounding streets to traffic. In what has become an annual event—equal parts political demonstration and Lenten procession—they set off marching in four orderly columns toward the cathedral, where an outdoor mass will be celebrated. Someone initiates a chant, which is quickly taken up by the marchers: *"Queremos obispos al lado de los pobres"* ("We want bishops who side with the poor").

Today, Romero is emblematic not only of the struggle for human rights, but also of the contributions to that struggle made by people of faith around the world. Whether in El Salvador or South Africa, Poland or India, Palestine or Tibet, the Philippines or Zimbabwe, South Korea or Burma (Myanmar), many human rights activists are religious people, who conceive their political efforts in distinctly religious terms.

Thousands of marchers have turned out, and their mood is celebratory rather than somber. Particularly striking is the presence of numerous young people, who were born in the three decades since Romero's death. As night falls, and the initial hum of cicadas develops into something more closely resembling the whine of a table saw, bottle rockets sizzle and explode overhead. But what best captures the spirit of the people is a spontaneous call-and-response chant: "*¡Romero vive! ¡La lucha sigue, sigue!*" ("Romero lives! The struggle continues!").

2

What Are Human Rights?

Courageous leaders such as Oscar Romero have helped to inspire new generations of human rights advocates, and the idea of human rights is today widely endorsed in principle. Yet, for many, human rights remain an elusive ideal rather than a practical reality. Moreover, as with any popular ideal, "human rights" is also a rhetorically loaded phrase, and its very ubiquity may conceal underlying ambiguities in its application. What exactly is a human right? How are rights related to obligations? Which moral or legal claims express genuine human rights?

In this chapter we attempt to sketch a rough map of these conceptual contours. Unlike the previous chapter, which focused on the practical struggle for human rights in Central America, this chapter examines the *concept* of human rights and its historical development.

Like maps of rivers, or of disputed territorial borders, our map is provisional and subject to revision. However, it may still be of some help in orienting oneself in this otherwise complex and shifting terrain.

Rights

So that we can better appreciate what is distinctive about the concept of human rights, it will be helpful to begin by examining the genus of which it is a species—namely, the notion of *rights.* Generally speaking, talk of rights involves at least three grammatical elements: a subject, a direct object, and an indirect object. Thus, we can speak of X's right to Y vis-à-vis Z, where X is the *bearer of a right,* Y represents the *content of the right* (what it is a right *to*), and Z is the *person or institution against whom the right is asserted.* For example, we can imagine a journalist asserting the right to freedom of the press against her government. Although, in any given case, X is a particular individual, X's right to Y is typically a function of this individual's membership in a larger group (for example, the citizenry of a liberal democracy). To assert a right is, in essence, to demand something to which one is entitled by virtue of being properly positioned or otherwise having met the relevant criteria.

Given these features of rights-talk, we can propose a rough definition of rights: your rights are entitlements pertaining to those needs and desires that other people are obligated to fulfill, or to allow *you* to fulfill. According to this account, rights have both a negative and a positive dimension: they can be violated by omission as well as by commission. It has become customary to express the normative force of rights by saying that *my rights entail others' duties*. However, this way of putting the point overlooks the fact that many rights take the form of liberties or immunities (freedoms *from*, rather than freedoms *to*) and so entail constraints or "disabilities," rather than positive duties, on the part of others. For example, I may have a right to place pink flamingo lawn ornaments in my yard, but it is not clear that this entails any specific duties for my neighbors, apart from the general obligation to respect my private property.

On the other hand, the notion of rights is meaningless if a person's rights do not make some sort of corresponding demand on the behavior of others. Imagine, for example, that I prefer a ten-foot radius of personal space when I go out in public. However, since other people are not obliged to respect this idiosyncratic preference of mine, I cannot be said to

have a *right* to what I want in this case. If
we use the term *obligations* broadly, so as to
include constraints as well as positive duties,
then it can properly be said that my rights
entail others' obligations.[1] According to this
formulation, obligations have to do with what
we owe to others, and rights have to do with
what others owe to us.

But although the terms are conceptually
related, talk of rights cannot simply be trans-
lated into talk of obligations, or vice versa. For
one thing, although rights entail obligations,
not all obligations entail rights. For example,
I may have a moral obligation to be generous toward others, but it does not follow that
any potential beneficiary of my generosity
has a *right* to it. This example helps to bring
out additional features of rights—namely, that
they pertain primarily to *individuals* and to
what they can legitimately expect from others
as their due.[2] As one scholar helpfully puts it,
rights-talk provides us with "a way of talking
about 'what is just' from a special angle: the
viewpoint of the 'other(s)' to whom something
is owed or due, and who would be wronged if
denied that something."[3] Moreover, by placing
the accent on individual entitlement, rather
than on some more abstract requirement of
justice, rights-talk is inherently minimalistic: it pertains to what is decent, rather than

to what is good. To put it another way, the obligations that an individual's rights create for others are not supererogatory. One who infringes upon another's rights or does not adequately address the demands they create is blameworthy, but like an employer who, in accordance with the terms of a contract, pays an employee the sum on which they had earlier freely agreed, one who respects the rights of others is not considered meritorious or worthy of any special praise.

The Idea of Human Rights

Many rights, such as the right to vote in presidential elections in the United States, are the product of distinctive political and legal arrangements and pertain only to the individuals who happen to belong to the relevant community (in this example, U.S. citizens of a certain age who legally reside in one of the fifty states). That this is so has led some theorists to suppose that rights are essentially government grants, and that the having of rights—not to mention the particular rights that one has—depends entirely upon one's membership in a given political community. In contrast to this view, which is a version of legal positivism, other thinkers have held that at least some rights are "natural"—that they do not depend upon any contingent feature of one's identity and so are possessed universally. The latter is the philosophical tradition out of which the contemporary idea of human rights emerged.

What the idea of human rights claims is that all human beings possess the same basic rights, irrespective of their other differences, and that these rights place human beings in a state of reciprocal obligation toward one another. In contrast to the sort of rights that must be earned, or that are available only to citizens of particular political communities, human rights are the common birthright of humanity, and their possession cannot depend on one's membership in any particular community (other than the human community itself). Having these rights is said to be a function of one's status as a human being, irrespective of one's culture, nationality, race, religion, and so on. Thus, as an initial (purely formal) definition, we can say that human rights are *rights belonging to every human being, which every (appropriately situated) human being is obligated to respect.*[4] Their universality cuts in both directions: everyone (it is claimed) owes something to everyone else. In practice, as we shall see, it is primarily (though not exclusively) against governments (as opposed to private individuals) that human rights are conceived as claimable.

Development

Although, as we shall see in chapter 5, human-rights thinking has important historical antecedents, the idea of human rights as we know it today is relatively recent. It came into prominence during the Enlightenment, as Europe was undergoing significant social changes.[5] In modernity, the institutions and social arrangements that were designed to protect basic human dignity in premodern societies broke down, and the individual was suddenly faced with unprecedented challenges to his or her ability to live a decent human life. As one scholar puts it, "Society, which once protected his dignity and provided him with an important place in the world, now appears, in the form of the modern state, the modern economy, and the modern city, as an alien power that assaults his dignity and that of his family."[6] The idea of human rights, and with it the conviction that the authority of the group is limited by the dignity of the individual, emerged partly in response to these distinctly modern challenges.

Modernity and the Enlightenment were also characterized by new attitudes toward authority and its justification, and traditional institutions and offices came increasingly to be viewed as suitable objects of criticism. The idea of human rights, with its presumption in favor of the individual, reflects new conceptions of political legitimacy and popular sovereignty. These developments, it is important to appreciate, affected not only the political philosophy of the time but also the political and social practices that philosophy takes as its starting point. Language derives its sense from practice, and the language of human rights is no exception. Thus, Annette Baier has observed that the development of the idea of human rights is associated not simply with, for example, the social contract theory of Locke and Rousseau but also—and more importantly—with an increasing unwillingness on the part of the powerless to beg from the powerful:

> The conditions of the form of human justice that recognizes universal rights include . . . a limited willingness to beg, a considerable unwillingness to ask, even when—if we did ask the powerful for a handout—it would perhaps be given to us. What we regard as ours by right is what we are unwilling to beg for and willing only within limits to say "thank you" for.[7]

In modernity, even charity—the highest of medieval virtues—was subjected to critical reappraisal, and the practice of asserting one's rights gradually came to replace the rituals of petitioning the powerful. A new conception of the self—as dignified bearer of inalienable rights—had emerged.[8]

Human Rights in the Twentieth Century

It was not until the mid-twentieth century, however, that talk of human rights entered into popular discourse. As before, developments in the language reflected developments in social conditions and practice. The twentieth century has been called the bloodiest in all of human history, and with good cause. With the rise of new ideologies, new social arrangements, and of course new (and lethal) technologies, human dignity was again under unprecedented assault.

Alluding to the horrors of the Holocaust and the Second World War (though without naming them), the preamble to the Universal Declaration of Human Rights observes, "Disregard and contempt for human rights have resulted in barbarous acts which have outraged the conscience of mankind." Arguably the most important moral manifesto to arise out of that outrage, the Universal Declaration was drafted in 1947 and 1948, and it was officially adopted by the United Nations on December 10, 1948.[9] It consists of thirty articles proclaimed to represent a "common standard of achievement for all peoples and all nations." The universality this implies is further reinforced by the language used in each of the articles: almost all of them begin with the word *everyone* or with the phrase *all human beings* (or *no one*, where immunities are at issue). The rights enumerated here are meant to apply globally, though it is worth noting that while no state voted against the declaration in the United Nations General Assembly, Saudi Arabia, South Africa, and the Soviet-bloc countries abstained. Despite its references to the barbarism of the recent past, the declaration is an optimistic document, which looks forward to "the advent of a world in which human beings shall enjoy freedom of speech and belief and freedom from fear and want."[10]

Among the rights listed in the declaration are the following:

- The right to life
- Freedom from slavery
- Freedom from torture
- The right to equal protection before the law
- Freedom of movement
- The right to own property
- Freedom of conscience and religion

- Freedom of assembly
- The right to work
- The right to an education

However, the declaration was not meant to be comprehensive or exhaustive. Rather, by articulating the aspirations of (at least much of) the international community, it set the stage for future international resolutions, conventions, covenants, treaties, and other human rights instruments.

Although it is not legally binding, the declaration is significant, among other reasons, insofar as it set in motion the emergence of a systematic body of international human rights law and the transformation of an essentially moral ideal into a political reality. To give legal weight to the rights enumerated in the Universal Declaration, in 1966 the United Nations adopted two additional treaties: the International Covenant on Civil and Political Rights (ICCPR) and the International Covenant on Economic, Social, and Cultural Rights (ICESCR), both of which came into effect in 1976. The former includes such rights as freedom of expression, the right to be presumed innocent until proven guilty, and the right to privacy; the latter includes, for example, the right to safe working conditions, the right to join trade unions, and the right to adequate food, clothing, and shelter. Taken together, the Universal Declaration, the ICCPR, and the ICESCR are known as the International Bill of Rights.

"Generations" of Human Rights

While it has generally proven politically advantageous to pay lip service to the idea of human rights, at least as long as the latter is conceived in fairly abstract terms, there has been much debate within the international community as to *which* putative rights are in fact genuine *human* rights, and some countries have refused to be bound by international human rights law. The United States did not ratify the ICCPR until 1992, and it has never ratified the ICESCR.[11]

Indeed, part of the explanation for the existence of these two distinct human rights covenants—one for civil and political rights and the other for economic, social, and cultural rights—is to be found in the differing priorities of Western liberal democracies and (what were once) Marxist states. Generally speaking, the ICCPR tended to reflect the concerns of the former, whereas the ICESCR tended to reflect the priorities of the latter. Since then, additional instruments have been created to address specific classes of people and issues not adequately covered in the International Bill of Rights, including conventions on the rights of women and children and a Declaration on the Right to Development.

Many commentators now speak of these developments as involving three "generations" of human rights. The first generation consists of civil and political rights such as the right to own property, freedom of speech, and the right to vote. The rights in this category are ones that human beings enjoy as individuals and that are asserted primarily in relation to their own governments. Thus, they reflect the important role played in most of the modern world by nation-states. They are called the first generation of human rights because their importance was recognized relatively early on (for example, by John Locke and by the drafters of the Declaration of Independence and the American Bill of Rights).

A second set of human rights includes several economic, social, and cultural rights, such as the right to an education and the right to earn a living. Unlike civil and political rights, second-generation rights are harder to protect, since they tend to involve positive entitlements rather than simply freedoms and immunities. Thus, their realization depends upon the existence of civil institutions such as schools, hospitals, and labor unions.[12] Moreover, unlike first-generation rights, which are typically asserted against one's own government, it is not always clear who is responsible for meeting the obligations that second-generation rights entail.

Currently, an international consensus is beginning to take shape regarding a third generation of human rights. These rights differ from the others insofar as they are generally rights that pertain to groups of human beings, rather than directly to individuals.[13] This is in part because—unlike torture or arbitrary arrest, say—the challenges to which they respond are ones that threaten more than just isolated individuals. Some examples of these proposed "group rights" are the right to peace, the right to a healthy environment, and the right to economic development.[14] Also very important to this category are the rights of minorities and indigenous communities.

Every declaration of rights is ultimately a product of its times, as notable for what it omits as for what it includes. For instance, the International Bill of Rights, while global in its aspirations, uses gendered language and makes no mention of sexual orientation; what it says about the family is clearly reflective of mid-twentieth-century Western social norms.

Thus, even if human rights themselves are universal, it is not surprising that the declarations in which they are articulated develop over time.

Enforcement and Prosecution

While the codification of international human rights law represents a major accomplishment of the past half century, the biggest impediment to the realization in practice of human rights remains the lack of adequate mechanisms for enforcement. At present, the primary guarantors of the rights enumerated in treaties such as the ICCPR and the ICESCR are the signatory states themselves—an arrangement that respects state sovereignty but results in considerable variation with respect to human rights practice within the international community. Many observers have noted the resulting paradox that "states are at one and the same time the necessary agents for the implementation of human rights, and also among their chief violators, or at least colluders in their violation."[15] The role played by the United Nations itself is largely supervisory. Its most important human rights body, the Human Rights Council, comprises representatives from various governments who are charged with examining allegations of human rights violations by states.[16] The UN's various other adjudicatory bodies, including the Human Rights Committee (in the case of the ICCPR) and the Committee on Economic, Social, and Cultural Rights (in the case of the ICESCR), can examine and record allegations of abuse reported by either states or individuals, but they cannot ordinarily initiate investigation or undertake action on their own. More often than not, the primary incentive for states to comply with international law is the pressure of public opinion rather than the threat of any more direct collective action.

Although, in the absence of an international "police force," the human rights legal regime lacks effective mechanisms for uniform enforcement, the past few years have seen the creation of a judiciary body charged with trying individuals accused of grievous violations of international law. Under the terms of an international treaty called the Rome Statute, the International Criminal Court (ICC) was established in The Hague to address "the most serious crimes of concern to the international community as a whole," namely genocide, crimes against humanity, war crimes, and the crime of aggression. The treaty was adopted by 120 states in 1998 and entered into force in 2002. While its jurisdiction is limited and

does not include many of the rights enumerated in prior declarations and treaties,
the ICC nevertheless represents a significant
stride toward the implementation of international human rights law. However, the United
States—which, along with China, Iraq (then
under Saddam Hussein), Israel, Libya, Qatar,
and Yemen, voted against the Rome Statute—
has expressed strong opposition to the ICC.[17]

Grassroots Organizations

Despite the ongoing challenges facing international law, the idea of human rights remains
an immensely attractive and powerful moral
ideal, as attested by the work of numerous
human rights nongovernmental organizations (NGOs) and grassroots groups. In recent
decades, the phrase *human rights* has become
associated closely with the work of Amnesty
International, Human Rights Watch, and
other such organizations. While employing
a staff of lawyers and human rights profes-
sionals, such organizations are also adept at
marshaling popular support for human rights.
By building networks among concerned vol-
unteers and financial contributors around the
world, they have helped to distribute the costs
(personal as well as financial) of human rights
activism. Amnesty International, which was

founded by British lawyer Peter Benenson in 1961, is famous for the letter-writing (and e-mail) campaigns it organizes on behalf of prisoners of conscience and other victims of human rights abuse, and chapters of the organization can be found on college campuses and in communities around the world.

The success of these grassroots efforts is indicative of the role that public opinion can play in such matters. The desire on the part of governments to avoid public embarrassment is often a powerful practical incentive to respect human rights—though it is also a fragile one that depends upon the continued prestige and legitimacy of the human rights ideal.

Continuing Development

This chapter has attempted a brief sketch of the history of the idea of human rights. But some skeptics deny the existence of universal human rights precisely on the ground that the idea of human rights *has* a history. One such skeptic, the prominent philosopher Alasdair MacIntyre, argues that rights "presuppose . . . the existence of a socially established set of rules. Such sets of rules only come into existence at particular historical periods under particular social circumstances. They are in no way universal features of the human condition."[18] According to MacIntyre, human rights "are fictions" comparable to "witches or unicorns."[19]

However, the fact that *thinking* about human rights has a history does not necessarily lead to the conclusion that rights themselves are merely historical artifacts or "constructs." It is true that one cannot talk of rights outside the social conditions that make such talk intelligible, but given those conditions of intelligibility, one can speak of rights existing in other times and places.[20] From within the particularity of a historical context, as we will argue more fully in chapter 4, it is possible to make claims that aspire to be true universally.

Human rights are said to obtain irrespective of time and place, but thinking about human rights—and the language in which this thought is expressed—is neither universal nor ahistorical. Like all moral discourse, it developed in a particular time and place, in response to various historical forces, and it depends for its sense upon the maintenance of certain practices. These are the *conditions* that make possible talk of *unconditional* rights.

As threats to human dignity change, the discourse and practice of human rights also must adapt. The past sixty years have seen the development of new ways of thinking about human rights and new institutions for protecting them. Nevertheless, enormous challenges remain. Whereas the infrastructure, if not the language, of human rights is best adapted to protecting the individual from his or her own government, in our contemporary, globalized world, threats to human dignity come increasingly from other sources (though governments continue to rank near the top of the list), ranging from multinational corporations to terrorist organizations. And as we have seen, these threats often endanger communities, not just particular individuals. Thus, the creation and maintenance of a global human rights regime will require new ways of holding all of us accountable to one another, both morally and legally.

3

Human Rights and the Problem of Grounding

"All human beings are born free and equal in dignity and rights. They are endowed with reason and conscience and should act towards one another in a spirit of brotherhood." These words from article 1 of the Universal Declaration of Human Rights express a truly remarkable claim: that irrespective of nationality, race or ethnicity, economic status, gender, sexual orientation, religion, social connections, and indeed any other diferentiating fact about ourselves, each and every one of us possesses dignity and is deserving of respect and kindness *just by virtue of being human.*

Notice, however, that the Universal Declaration of Human Rights is silent about the source of this dignity that persons possess. As the prominent Muslim scholar of human rights Abdullahi Ahmed An-Naʻim notes,

"The omission of any specific foundation of the equality of all human beings in dignity and rights, whether religious or secular, was apparently designed to evade the issue in the interest of achieving consensus on the Declaration." But today more than ever, An-Na'im adds, "the question of the moral or philosophical foundation of human rights remains both difficult to answer and critical for the practical implementation of these rights."[1]

For critics of human rights, the declaration's silence on the question of foundations is evidence that its moral claims are baseless—that no such foundations exist. Thus, Alasdair MacIntyre scathingly remarks, "In the United Nations declaration on human rights of 1949 [sic] what has since become the normal U.N. practice of not giving good reasons for any assertions whatsoever is followed with great rigour."[2] This chapter does not attempt to offer good reasons for the assertion about human dignity with which it begins; however, it explores the prior question of what these grounds might look like—of the form that a justification of human dignity (and derivatively, of human rights) might take. Later chapters are then devoted to the task of sketching the outline of such an account.

Moral Justification: The Very Idea

The assumption behind MacIntyre's gibe is that moral claims deserve our respect and allegiance only if they can be furnished with good grounds. What we need, he suggests, are *reasons* for caring about one another. But that this is so is not itself obvious. Let's imagine that a person has collapsed in an airport terminal. Others quickly rush to his or her aid. We may admire these individuals, even call them heroes for saving the day, but we do not ordinarily consider their behavior to stand in need of justification. Rather, it is the person who strides past without stopping to help from whom we demand (or would like to demand) some explanation. "What's wrong with him?" one might ask of such a person, thus implying that his lack of concern constitutes a defect of character, a lack of human wholeness.

There is indeed something important to appreciate here, and it has to do with the fact that instinctive, prereflective reactions play a fundamental role in our thinking about moral matters. Ludwig Wittgenstein once remarked, "My attitude towards him is an attitude towards a soul. I am not of the *opinion* that he has a soul."[3] He meant that our recognition of the humanity of others shows itself in how we respond to them, and that these reactions are not themselves the result of a prior "theory" we have chosen to adopt on independent grounds. Of course, morality involves rational deliberation, but our moral reactions to others provide the conditions within which such deliberation–including the demand for justification–has its sense and gravity.

In fact, one reason for treating certain moral claims with skepticism is precisely that they do not accord with, or allow us to make sense of, our untutored moral intuitions. For instance, some animal rights activists use the slogan "Meat is murder." The force of such a remark derives from the way we ordinarily employ the concept of *murder*: it draws an analogy between the slaughter of animals for food and the slaughter of other human beings. But can those who use this slogan really mean what they say? Our moral reactions seem to belie such claims.[4] One's reaction to a chicken or a fish is simply not a reaction to a soul (a point that has nothing to do with any "theory" of what a soul is)–which is not to say that it is a reaction to an insentient piece of matter either.[5]

The point here is that our sense of human dignity is closely related to how we actually respond to other human beings. But how ought we to conceive of this relation? One possibility would be to say that human beings have dignity *because* (or *insofar as*) we respond to them with respect. The eminent legal theorist Ronald Dworkin seems to endorse a version of this argument when he writes:

> The life of a single human organism commands respect and protection . . . because of the complex creative investment it represents and because of our wonder at the . . . processes that produce new lives from old ones, at the processes of nation and community and language . . . , and, finally . . . at the process of internal personal creation and judgment.[6]

On this account, the "sacredness" of human beings is a function of the wonder and awe they inspire in us.[7]

However, Michael Perry argues that such a view of the relation between our understanding of human dignity and our reactions is inadequate as the basis for human-rights thinking. Perry, a Catholic legal scholar and philosopher, does not dispute Dworkin's claim that human beings can be awe inspiring or his claim that they are sacred; however, he questions Dworkin's attempt to derive the latter from the former. He writes, "To suggest . . . that something is sacred *because* it inspires awe in us, because we value it, is to reverse the ordinary order of things."[8] Perry continues:

> Dworkin seems to be using "sacred" in what we can call a weak, or "subjective," sense—something (for example, a human life) is sacred *because*, or *in the sense that*, it inspires awe in us and we attach great value to it—rather than in the strong, or "objective," sense—something is sacred and *therefore* inspires awe in us and we attach great value to it.[9]

For Perry, reactions alone are too subjective a basis on which to build a conception of human dignity. For what are we to say about those who do not react as we think they should—who react, for instance, with contempt toward those who differ in some way from themselves? For Perry, it is important to affirm that human beings are sacred in an objective sense, so that their sacredness can function as a *reason* for treating them with respect.

Here, then, is a philosophical puzzle: If we say human dignity depends entirely on human reactions, then we forfeit the grounds required for claiming that human beings *ought* to be treated with respect (irrespective of how they actually *are* treated). But if we say that human dignity is independent of and logically prior to human reactions, such that the latter must answer to the former, then it is not clear how such a conception of dignity could be rendered intelligible and defended. It would float free of our intuitions in much the same way that the claim that "meat is murder" does. In order to resolve this dilemma, it will be helpful to think further about our moral reactions and how they differ from purely physiological responses.

Instincts: Moral and Physiological

Charles Taylor has noted that certain moral reactions, including the inclination to come to the aid of those who are injured, are "uncommonly deep, powerful, and universal."[10] But although apparently "instinctual," such reactions are also shaped by one's culture. Thus, while the demand to render assistance is felt in all cultures, there can be—and in fact is—disagreement among (and even within) cultures as to the scope of what is demanded of one: Does the obligation extend only to members of one's own caste, tribe, race, religion, and so on? Or is the class of beneficiaries wider? (This is, of course, the question famously posed by the parable of the good Samaritan.) Whatever answer is given, Taylor notes, will be "inseparable from an account of what it is that commands our respect."[11] It will serve in effect to pick out those properties of persons that are thought to render them deserving of our attention and concern. Our moral reactions are thus "not only 'gut' feelings but also implicit acknowledgments of claims concerning their objects."[12] They entail what Taylor calls an "ontology of the human," an account of what it is that merits our response.[13]

In this respect, our moral reactions differ from mere physiological responses such as nausea. To be sure, both are reactions to objects possessing certain properties, but "in one case the property marks the object as one *meriting* this reaction; in the other the connection between the two is just a brute fact."[14] For instance, there is no point in arguing over which objects or states of affairs *ought* to evoke nausea. There might be ways of manipulating such responses, as in *A Clockwork Orange*, but "what seems to make no sense here is the supposition that we might articulate a description of the nauseating in terms of its intrinsic properties, and then argue from this that certain things which we in fact react to that way are not really fit objects for it," or that certain things we do not find nauseating really are.[15] The concept of *the nauseating* is simply coterminous with whatever in fact elicits nausea.

Earlier we noted Perry's concern that making human dignity (or "sacredness") depend on our reactions—as he thinks Dworkin's argument does—reverses the natural order of things. Perry's worry is that appealing to moral reactions will render dignity as subjective a concept as the nauseating. But Taylor's point is that moral reactions need not be understood on the model of purely physiological responses. In the case of the former, but not the latter, it is possible to *argue* about which reactions are merited and which are not. The ontological claims implicit in (or affirmed by) our moral responses open up a space for critical reflection and debate.

On Taylor's account, dignity and moral reactions are closely intertwined, but neither is more basic than the other. It is impossible to make sense of or debate the claims of human ontology without relying on our reactions, and vice versa. Because our moral reactions are not simply brute facts—because they can be reasoned about and need not merely be accepted as given—it is sometimes necessary to suppress certain reactions in the interests of the claims implicit in others. Our reactions are not, after all, infallible. But although they can be refined, our reactions cannot be dispensed with, in the service of a more "rational" moral calculus. For without such reactions, moral reflection would simply not be possible. As Taylor notes, "It is never a question of prescinding from our reactions altogether," of attempting to construct an ontology of the human from a neutral, disinterested stance, unencumbered by moral instinct.[16] For our instincts are "our mode of access to the world in which ontological claims are discernible and can be rationally argued about and sifted."[17] To ignore them is to lose sight of the very thing we purport to be arguing about.[18]

Ontologies of the Human and the Grounds of Dignity

Philosophers have wondered what reasons can be given in answer to the question of why we ought to care about one another. But truly asking such a question—for example, when stepping over an injured person on the way to the departure lounge—is pathological. An individual unfettered by moral instincts, and so without an ontology of the human, is a person bereft of all moral direction, with whom there consequently would be little hope of reasoning about moral matters. Competent moral agents, by contrast, are already inside the space of moral reflection, relying on certain moral reactions even as they criticize others.

Moral reactions can be distinguished from purely physiological responses in part because they entail ontological commitments. These commitments are deeply embedded in our thinking, and as Taylor notes, "The moral ontology behind any person's views can remain largely implicit."[19] However, when what is implicit is made explicit in the form of a claim, it can be rationally examined and debated.[20] To attempt to articulate grounds for treating others with compassion and respect is thus to seek to make explicit an appropriate ontology of the human—a conception of human nature such that these human beings are seen as *meriting* our concern. This is a task properly undertaken in dialogue with others, drawing upon the full range of critical resources that our traditions make available to us. The challenge here is addressed not to sociopaths who are devoid of moral insight, but to ordinary human beings like ourselves, who respond in characteristic ways to others. Thus, any such justification will be rooted in our reactions, even though the claims implicit in these reactions will need to be scrutinized, debated, and refined—in some cases necessitating adjustments in the reactions themselves. The goal of this process of mutual correction is what John Rawls has described as a state of "reflective equilibrium."[21]

An ontology of the human is an account of what it is about human beings—or about certain human beings—that merits our respect. But such accounts can vary both among and within traditions. At one extreme, the property picked out may serve to define a privileged class of human beings (for example, landholding European men). But the account can also be broader in scope. Such an account might tell us, for instance, that all human beings "are creatures of God and made in his image, or that they are immortal souls, or that they are . . . emanations of divine fire, or that they are . . . rational agents and thus have a dignity which transcends any other being, or some other such characterization; and that *therefore* we owe them respect."[22]

We began by raising the question of the grounds for human rights. Now we can return to that question with a clearer understanding of what we are asking. To inquire into the grounds for human rights is to raise the question of the sort of human ontology compatible with the claim with which this chapter began: that all human beings are born free and equal in dignity and rights and should treat one another like brothers and sisters. Although every ontology derives its significance from the tradition(s) out of which it develops, the properties identified by the relevant sort of ontology would be universal, unrestricted by race, gender, nationality, religion, or any other social division.

Perry has argued that only religion is capable of providing us with an *objective* conception of human dignity (or sacredness), and that, consequently, the idea of human rights—that there are certain things that ought to be done for all human beings, and other things that ought never to be done to them—is "ineliminably religious."[23] We agree that religious traditions can make available ontologies of the human that conform to the requirements just articulated. However, we see no reason to deny that similar resources can be found within other, nonreligious traditions of moral reflection.[24]

In chapter 6 we will attempt to offer our own rudimentary account of human dignity—one grounded in religious claims distinctive of the Christian tradition. But we do not claim that ours is the only such account that can be offered. Other accounts, other ontologies of the human, can be articulated from within other traditions (religious and nonreligious), and even from within Christianity itself. Indeed, as we will try to show in the next chapter, it is not necessary to achieve consensus at the level of ontology in order to be justified in affirming the universality of human dignity.

Dignity: Human or Divine?

By placing the emphasis on *human personhood*–albeit personhood as understood from within the context of particular moral and religious traditions–the approach we advocate differs from certain other ways of thinking about the relation between religion and human rights that claim to derive such rights from divine commands or a universal moral law. Such proposals ultimately seek to locate the source of human rights in something other than the inherent worth–the sacredness–of individual human beings themselves (for example, in the will of God or the laws of nature). However, insofar as they place the object of moral respect somewhere outside human beings themselves, these accounts are better suited to talk of duties than to talk of inherent rights. Respect for human beings is rendered a by-product of respect for something "higher."

Jeffrey Stout has recently argued that the idea of a natural law is best understood as an "imaginative projection," the point of which is to underscore the need for ongoing social criticism.[25] The "law" is that *toward which* we are feeling, rather than that *from which* we are currently in a position to argue.[26] The task of articulating human rights would no doubt be easier–even otiose–if we could simply crib from the eternal law; but unfortunately that is not an option for earthbound humans. By grounding human rights in human dignity, the view for which we are arguing need not offer any particular account of which claims express genuine human rights. That is a question that must be discussed and debated, as indeed it continues to be. And as we saw in chapter 2, the answers that are given change over time, as social conditions evolve. But religious traditions can contribute to this process insofar as they provide resources for affirming the dignity of all human beings.

4

Universal Human Rights and Religious Particularity

A ny attempt to offer a religious justification for human rights—to ground the idea
of human rights from within one or another
religious tradition—must come to terms with
an apparent antinomy: the claims of human
rights are *universal* in scope and purport to
be universally valid, whereas religions are
particular. To put it another way, the possession of human rights, by definition, cannot
depend on one's membership in any particular community (apart from the human community itself), but religion, by its very nature,
is rooted in the histories, narratives, and
practices of determinate communities of the
faithful—communities that frequently define
themselves (at least partially) in opposition to
one another. In yet a third formulation of this
apparent paradox, every individual is said to
possess the *same* basic human rights, whereas

religion is inherently *pluralistic*, and not all individuals possess the same religious commitments, if indeed they possess any such commitments at all. The question, then, is whether the universality inherent in the concept of human rights can be reconciled with the particularity and plurality of the determinate religious faiths.

For many contemporary theorists, the answer is unequivocally negative. For example, the distinguished scholar Louis Henkin has argued, "Human rights are not, and cannot be, grounded in religious conviction."[1] As Henkin sees it, human rights are universal in scope and application and therefore require universally accessible support. The effort, even by well-meaning religious thinkers, to ground such rights in one or another set of distinctive faith commitments is "conceptually imperialistic."[2] Henkin concludes:

> For the human rights movement, universal human rights cannot rest on theistic foundations. Such supports are not available, or acceptable, to those who cannot share theistic assumptions. . . . In the end, and at bottom, for the human rights movement insistence on the nontheistic foundations of the contemporary human rights idea reflects a quest for universal acceptance and universal commitment to a common moral intuition articulated in specific agreed-upon terms.[3]

Although Henkin here speaks of *theistic* assumptions, it is clear that his point is meant to apply to religion in general: since not everyone shares (the same) religious beliefs, whether theistic or not, and since the idea of human rights is meant to be universal in its purview, the success of the latter "depends on its secularity and rationality."[4] Thus, for Henkin, human rights and religion fall on opposite sides of a public-private dichotomy.

Implicit in these remarks are two distinct but related concerns, which it is important to distinguish. The first has to do with the *justification* of the human rights idea and its public accessibility, and the second concerns its *validity* or *truth*. The worry about justification is that if the idea of human rights can coherently be supported only from within the context of some particular religion (or of "religion" in some broader sense), then there will necessarily be many people (those who are not "religious," or who do not participate in the relevant faith community) for whom the idea cannot be justified and who therefore cannot coherently give themselves to the cause of human rights. Thus, Henkin writes elsewhere that since "the human rights idea aspires to universalism . . . it needs a base that has universal appeal."[5] By seeking to ground the idea of human rights in one or another religion, religious theorists—however well intentioned—are in effect limiting the appeal of an idea that, according to Henkin, ought to be acceptable to all, irrespective of religion or the lack thereof.

The second concern is related to the first, but for us to understand this relation, a brief detour into moral theory will prove helpful. Consider the following three philosophical positions:

1. The first, which we can call *moral objectivism*, is the view that there are moral truths that hold quite independently of whether or not they are endorsed by oneself or one's community. According to this account, morality is more than simply convention or invention, and here, as elsewhere, believing something does not make it so. Notably, while the moral objectivist maintains that there are moral truths to be known, she need not claim that she (or anyone else) knows (in their totality) what these truths are. Objectivism is perfectly compatible with fallibilism and with the acknowledgment of a plurality of moral traditions and competing points of view.

2. The second position is *moral relativism*. The relativist argues that what is right and wrong differs from one culture (or even individual) to another, such that the *very same act*

could be right in one context and wrong in another. Relativism has little difficulty accommodating cultural plurality (though it does so by the paradoxical strategy of denying the reality of cross-cultural disagreement), but insofar as it rejects universality altogether, it is plainly incompatible with the idea of universal human rights.

3. The third position, which is sometimes called *moral constructivism*, seeks to mediate between moral objectivism and moral relativism. Like the relativist, the constructivist regards morality as a human construct. However, like the objectivist (and unlike the relativist), the constructivist believes that moral norms can nevertheless be universally valid. According to constructivism, the validity of a candidate moral norm depends upon its universal acceptability. The only universally valid norms are ones that all human beings can—and under idealized conditions will—accept, in light of their shared interests.

Moral constructivism has many adherents among contemporary theorists of human rights—and, indeed, among moral theorists generally. The appeal of the theory is that it manages to make sense of the universality inherent in the concept of human rights without appealing to anything beyond basic human needs and desires. Moreover, it also entails that moral knowledge is possible and comparatively easy to come by. Whereas the moral objectivist sees the justification of a moral belief, however widely admitted, as merely *pointing toward* its truth, the constructivist sees "moral truth" or validity as *constituted by* (universal) acceptance.[6] However, it also should be clear that, given such a view, the attempt to ground human rights in religion is unlikely to appear very promising. By equating the validity of a moral norm with its ability to command universal assent, constructivism cannot regard as valid any norm whose justification depends upon the prior acceptance of a distinctive (and contested) set of religious commitments.[7] Given a constructivist view of moral validity, then, the two concerns implicit in Henkin's remarks—and in similar objections to the attempt to ground human rights in religion—are closely connected.

Universality and Justification

In the foregoing discussion, we have been speaking of universality (or the lack thereof) in at least three different ways. In one sense, a norm may be said to be universal if it pertains to *all human beings*, either because it makes demands *on* all human beings or because it places one under a responsibility *to* all human beings (or, as is typically the case with respect to human rights, both). In a second sense, a norm may be said to be universal if it is binding *at all times and in all places.* In the third sense, a norm may be said to be universal if it commands sufficiently widespread (that is, universal) *acceptance.* The first—universality of scope—is to some degree a grammatical question, to be answered by reference to the size of the norm's intended audience and the nature of the demands made on it. Whether or not a norm is universal in the second sense is an essentially normative (or evaluative) question, equivalent to inquiring into its validity. Universality in the third sense—universal acceptability—is a sociological matter, to be ascertained by empirical means.

A command like "Thou shalt not kill" is universal in the first sense, because it is implicitly unrestricted with respect to both its grammatical subject (thou) and its implied object (anyone).[8] It also aspires to universality in the second sense, insofar as it purports to be valid everywhere and at all times. However, history suggests that it is not universal in the third sense; at any rate, it is easy to imagine disagreement about its practical application.

On a constructivist view of moral validity, the implications of this fact may be troubling, since universality in the second sense (universal validity) is thought to depend on universality in the third sense (universal acceptability). Moral constructivists of course have various resources at their disposal for addressing this worry—for example, the distinction between the *actual* conditions of justification (in which universal acceptance may indeed prove elusive) and *idealized* conditions (in which some of the practical impediments to consensus are removed). However, the quest for a more robust conception of morality might also incline one toward some version of objectivism.

We have argued elsewhere against moral constructivism and in favor of the objectivity of morality.[9] Although space does not permit us to rehearse those arguments here, it is worth noting that one weakness of the constructivist view is that it requires a strict formal partition between moral discourse and other forms of discourse, whereas one of the strengths of moral objectivism is that no such demarcation is required.[10] In each case, the objectivist insists, our aim is to bring our claims in line with what they are about.[11]

The kind of moral epistemology to which we are partial recognizes, with relativism, that moral reasoning takes place within particular moral traditions and that agents occupying different traditions may draw different conclusions about how human beings ought to behave.[12] Thus, it acknowledges that disagreement is a characteristic feature of moral discourse. But it argues, against relativism, that such disagreement presupposes there is indeed something worth debating—namely, moral truth. When coupled with moral objectivism, it thus allows for the affirmation of norms that are universal in both the first and second senses, even though such norms may not be universal in the third sense. In this way, it holds, pace constructivism, that *universal* validity can be affirmed from within *particular* contexts of justification. The term we will use in reference to this strategy for reconciling universality (at the level of norms) with particularity (at the level of justificatory contexts) is *situated universalism.*

Dignity and the Universality of Human Rights

Numerous theorists, of both religious and non-religious persuasions, have argued that the core idea of human rights is human dignity.[13] This view is affirmed as well in the preamble to the Universal Declaration of Human Rights, which speaks of "the inherent dignity . . . of all members of the human family" and of "the dignity and worth of the human person." To say that a person is the bearer of dignity is (at least) to say that she possesses *noninstrumental value.* Her worth does not depend on her utility to others; rather (to use Kantian language), she is an "end in herself." While people may disagree about which moral claims express valid human rights, all such discourse seems to depend on the acknowledgment of human dignity. In this way, dignity serves as the scaffold in terms on which the more specific claims of human rights can be elaborated and provided with a moral rationale.

Nevertheless, human dignity and human rights are not identical notions. Jack Donnelly helps to bring this out by asking us to imagine a society in which dignity is affirmed and maintained but that lacks the concept and practice of human rights. Consider, for example, a "relatively decentralized, non-bureaucratic, communitarian society," such as a tribal group:

> In such a society, the individual lacks many, if not most, of the rights that are so highly valued in the liberal democratic state. However, he has a secure and significant place in his society and has available a wide range

of intense personal and social relationships.
. . . He also has available regularized social
protections of many of the values and interests which in the West are protected through
individual human and legal rights. . . . Such
a society is undeniably morally defensible,
is in many ways quite attractive, and can be
said to protect basic human dignity.[14]

In certain cases, such a society—in which the
maintenance of one's dignity as a person and
perhaps even one's very survival depend on
one's continued membership in the larger
community—might be more effective than our
own at protecting the dignity of its members.
The latter might be puzzled, or even scandal-
ized, by the priority that we attach to the individual vis-à-vis her community and by the
claim that an individual can assert her dignity
over against the community of which she is a
part. But that is because they lack something
we possess—namely, the concept of individual
human rights.

Donnelly argues that whereas the idea of
human dignity is very old and can be found
in some form or other in nearly all civili-
zations, the concept of human rights is a
relatively recent idea, which came into prominence in Europe during the Enlightenment.
Its emergence in that time and place was not

accidental, for as we saw in chapter 2, under conditions of modernity, the individual was faced with unprecedented challenges to her dignity.

One of the principal ways in which the idea of human rights can be distinguished from other conceptions of human dignity is by its insistence that one's dignity as a person does not depend (entirely) on one's membership in any particular community. The possession of rights, according to this way of thinking, is a function of one's status as a human being, irrespective of one's culture, nationality, race, gender, religion, and so on. The idea of human rights is thus universal in the first of the three senses distinguished earlier: it entails the dignity of *all* human beings (and so imposes demands and/or constraints on all human beings). But is it also universal in the second sense, that of being universally valid? Notice that, according to both relativism and constructivism, the answer to this question hinges on whether or not the idea of human rights is one with which all will agree. If Donnelly is correct in claiming that there are cultures and ways of life to which the idea of human rights is foreign—and this certainly seems undeniable—then the prospects for justifying such an idea may appear problematic.

This is the conclusion at which Adamantia Pollis and Peter Schwab arrive, in a well-known essay entitled "Human Rights: A Western Construct with Limited Applicability." The title of their essay is indicative of the direction in which its argument moves: the development of the concept of human rights "can be traced to the particular experiences of England, France, and the United States" and, consequently, the concept of human rights is "irrelevant" in the non-Western world.[15] Pollis and Schwab claim, in short, that because the concept of human rights is not universally available or endorsed, it cannot be universally valid (which is equivalent to denying its validity altogether).

However, that conclusion can be avoided on an objectivist reading of our human rights discourse. According to the view outlined earlier, which we have termed *situated universalism*, it is unnecessary to achieve universal consensus on the idea of human rights in order to be justified in asserting that all human beings possess such rights. What *is* necessary is that one occupy a moral tradition from within which human beings are conceived of in the relevant way—that is, as possessing dignity qua human beings, rather than simply by virtue of their participation in a given community.[16] Let us call such a view of human dignity a *conception of universal human dignity*. The crucial point, in light of our present concern, is that a conception of universal human dignity need not be a *universal conception*, one held universally (or with which all others would agree). While a conception of universal human dignity is available only to those who participate in the relevant kind of community of discourse and practice (those with a suitable ontology of the human), the claims made possible in light of such a conception may be universal in scope, and their validity need not be threatened by the sheer fact that not everyone participates in the justificatory practices of the community in question.[17]

Although much contemporary theorizing about human rights seems to assume a constructivist view of moral validity (perhaps because of the tendency to model the moral dimensions of human rights discourse on its legal dimensions), it seems to us that the core idea of human rights in fact allies itself most naturally with the objectivist view. According to the latter, one's basic rights as a person, whatever they may be, do not depend on popular consensus and cannot be revoked by popular demand.

Plurality and Multiple Justifications

Earlier we noted two concerns raised by critics of the effort to ground the idea of human rights in religion: the first had to do with justification and its publicity, and the second with truth or validity. Thus far we have been focusing on the second of these concerns. We have maintained, against constructivism, that the validity of the idea of human rights does not depend on universal consensus and can be affirmed from within the particularity of a determinate moral tradition. Nevertheless, since the realization in practice of human dignity requires a supportive social environment, widespread endorsement of the idea of human rights is clearly desirable. If a rational justification for human rights is available only to those within a particular community, then such support is likely to be severely limited, to the detriment of the enjoyment of such rights by all. The problem, in other words, is *not* that without popular support for the idea of human rights, such rights would not exist; as we have seen, situated universalism holds that the dignity of all human beings and the consequent demands this dignity creates for all human beings can be affirmed from within a nonuniversal context of justification. Rather, the problem is that without such support, they would be virtually impossible to implement widely in practice.[18]

Here, then, we must return our attention to the first concern: the problem of the publicity of justification. In the remarks quoted earlier, Henkin objects to grounding human rights in religion for what we might describe as *formal* reasons—reasons pertaining to the form, rather than the content, of religious belief.[19] His concern, as we have seen, is that religious reasons for supporting human rights "are not available, or acceptable, to those who cannot share theistic [that is, religious] assumptions." In effect, Henkin is objecting not simply to *religious* foundations, nor to specifically *theistic* ones, but to any justification that is not universally available because it is rooted in what John Rawls calls a "comprehensive doctrine," that is, a particular worldview not shared by all.[20] This is what Henkin intends to rule out when he speaks of "a quest for universal acceptance and universal commitment to a common moral intuition *articulated in specific agreed-upon terms.*"

Whether any such persuasive secular justification—a justification neutral among competing visions of reality and humanity's place in it—can be furnished is itself the subject of widespread disagreement. Some thinkers, including Michael Perry, have argued that the idea of human rights is "ineliminably religious," and that "there is, finally, no intelligible secular version of the idea of human rights."[21] Personally, we do not find Perry's arguments in support of this claim entirely convincing, and in any case, our aim here is much more modest: to show not that a religious justification is necessary, but simply that it is not impossible.[22] However, even those who are equally committed to the idea of human rights do not necessarily articulate the grounds of their conviction in "specific agreed-upon terms." In contrast to what Henkin seems to assume, we would like to suggest that, when it comes to justification, such diversity is a strength, rather than a weakness.

Although, as we have argued, the implementation of human rights in practice requires (among other things) that everyone (or as many as possible) occupy a moral tradition from within which universal human dignity can be affirmed, it does not follow that all need to occupy the *same* moral tradition. Henkin's objection overlooks the possibility of multiple justifications for the idea of human rights.[23] From the point of view of our present discussion, a *plurality* of *particular* justifications for the idea of human rights is as good as a single widely shared justification. Moreover, since attempts to furnish the latter have not proved as successful as might have been hoped, the former approach—proceeding, as it were, from the bottom up, rather than from the top down—may ultimately turn out to be more fruitful. The hope is that, given a plurality of particular conceptions of universal human dignity, members of varying traditions might be able rationally to affirm one another's mutual dignity and basic rights as persons.

Of course, given the differences among these traditions, members of varying traditions may have varying understandings of how human dignity ought to be honored, and thus of which moral claims express valid human rights. But moral practice is not completely arbitrary, and it is likely that they will agree that certain specific acts—torture, slavery, genocide, and so on—are incompatible with human dignity, whatever else their conception of dignity might entail. Note, too, that the particularities of the contexts in which human rights claims are justified need not enter into the *content* of the claims themselves. It should be added that the aim of cross-cultural dialogue—and of human rights declarations, including the Universal Declaration of Human Rights—is not to replace the various richly textured moral traditions that human beings actually inhabit with a single, decontextualized "global ethic"; indeed, that effort would almost certainly prove disastrous. Rather, the aim is to identify and protect those specific freedoms on which there is general consensus across varying moral traditions and without which moral agency itself would be threatened.[24] As Henkin has rightly observed, these commonly accepted human rights constitute a "floor," not a "ceiling," representing a baseline of human decency, rather than humanity's highest moral aspirations.[25]

Theology and Universal Human Dignity

The plausibility of the claim that human beings have inalienable rights depends in large part upon one's conception of what it means to be human (one's ontology of the human), and not every conceivable understanding of human nature, or even of human dignity, is compatible with it. Now, some of the richest ontologies of the human can be found in religious traditions, which typically have encouraged deep reflection on this question. For better or worse, religions tend to embody claims about human nature as such, and one need not endorse Feuerbach's reduction of theology to anthropology in order to appreciate the intimacy of the relationship between reflection on the divine and reflection on the human. Religion is thus a natural resource for—and has contributed in various ways to—the development of humanistic moral visions.

Still, it must openly and frankly be acknowledged that religion has also been—and indeed remains—deeply implicated in habits of thought and patterns of behavior antithetical to the claims of human dignity. Religious believers have been among the world's worst abusers of human rights, and the good done in the name of religion can hardly atone for the evil. When looked at from a sociological or historical perspective, religion is clearly an ambiguous institution, if indeed it is a discrete category at all.

In recent years, the conception of religious studies as a purely descriptive discipline—and of the "world religions" as natural kinds, each with its own distinctive essence—has been challenged, and scholars of religion have been forced to acknowledge that their work is not as value-neutral as they had previously supposed. Often, however, the relation between human rights and the various religions is still approached as if it involved a purely descriptive question that could be given a disinterested answer. But to the extent that they harbor unacknowledged assumptions about what constitutes "authentic" Judaism, Islam, Buddhism, and so on, these efforts (often by outsiders) to "speak for" the so-called world religions are latently normative.[26]

For this reason, the task of articulating religious justifications for the idea of human rights remains properly *theological*—a task best undertaken conscious of one's commitments, from within one's own tradition, as one understands it. Theology seeks to remain faithful to the spirit of the tradition in which it is practiced, but since discerning that spirit is itself an interpretive act, requiring the hermeneutical retrieval of what one regards as deepest and most authentic, theology is necessarily also a self-critical, constructive, and transformative enterprise.[27] While it is therefore well beyond our capacity and right to attempt to ground the idea of human rights in traditions other than our own, we would like to highlight very briefly three contemporary examples of how this task is currently being undertaken by those scholars and activists for whom it *is* a proper endeavor.

One of the most creative religious theorists of human rights today is the Sudanese scholar Abdullahi Ahmed An-Na'im. A Muslim, An-Na'im argues that Shari'a (Islamic law) is a human construct, reflective of the social location in which it was formulated and the concerns of those who formulated it, and should not be equated with Islam itself.[28] Instead, An-Na'im recommends a return to the traditional *sources* of Shari'a, particularly the Qur'an and the Sunna (the customs of the Prophet), in an effort to rethink their moral significance and implications in an increasingly secularized and religiously pluralistic world. Consistent with the situated universalism we have been recommending here, An-Na'im believes that Islam, despite its particularity, can furnish its adherents with the resources necessary to affirm the dignity of all, Muslim and non-Muslim alike.[29]

Within Judaism, advocates of human rights often point to the Torah's claim that human beings are created *b'tselem Elohim* ("in the image of God").[30] It is this same conception of universal human dignity to which the signatories of a "Rabbinic Letter on Torture" addressed to President George W. Bush and members of the U.S. Congress appealed in 2005:

> We understand that the most fundamental ethical principle, which results from our belief in God as Creator of the world and Parent of all humanity, is that every human being is seen as reflecting the Image of God. Torture shatters and defiles God's Image.[31]

While deeply rooted in the Jewish tradition, the doctrine that human beings reflect the divine image and so, despite other differences, participate in a common humanity provides religious Jews with a conception of human nature as such—one that is understood as entailing ethical obligations even toward aliens, strangers, and enemies.[32] Moreover, as a variety of commentators has argued, this common humanity is understood within the rabbinic tradition as compatible with—and perhaps even entailing—human individuality and uniqueness.[33]

Among Buddhist ethicists, there is at present a lively debate over Buddhism's compatibility with the idea of human rights. Those who question their congruence point to the Buddha's denial of any enduring "self" and to Buddhism's apparent rejection (as based on just such an illusory notion of selfhood) of Western conceptions of entitlement.[34] Moreover, overtly theistic efforts to ground human dignity, such as the Jewish view just outlined, are naturally problematic in a Buddhist context. Nevertheless, many Buddhist thinkers claim that Buddhism can and does furnish its adherents with a conception of universal human dignity—one grounded not in "Western" notions of autonomous selfhood but in a distinctively Buddhist

understanding of personhood. According to
Damien Keown, for example, human dignity is
reflective of the universal capacity for enlightenment, the "Buddha-nature":

> Buddhism teaches that we are all poten-
> tial Buddhas. . . . By virtue of this common
> potential for enlightenment, all individuals
> are worthy of respect, and justice therefore
> demands that the rights of each individual
> must be protected.[35]

It is worth noting, in this connection, that
the two Buddhists to have received the Nobel
Peace Prize—the Fourteenth Dalai Lama and
Aung San Suu Kyi—are both human rights
activists, and that both are distinguished by
(among other things) the remarkable way in
which they refuse to place those who oppose
them outside the circle of humanity.

Keith Ward has observed, "The differences
between religious traditions are nowhere
clearer than in their views of human nature."[36]
This diversity might naturally be supposed to
diminish the prospects for a common commitment to the core idea of human rights.
Yet, as we have tried to show, a diversity of
distinctive perspectives on human nature is
not in itself incompatible with the reciprocal affirmation of universal human dignity.
In each of the cases we have described, and

in many more that we have not, a conception of *universal* human dignity is nourished
by resources internal to a *particular* tradition.
Moreover—and perhaps contrary to what one
might expect, given Henkin's view—it seems
that the strongest case for universality typically derives from what is "thickest" and most
distinctive about each tradition, rather than
from their least common denominator. Thus,
as long as the world's religions remain a primary source of moral insight for many (if not
most) people, members of varying traditions
who value human rights might effectively
work in concert with one another, each seeking support for the idea of human rights in
the tradition of which she or he is a part.[37] In
this way, the reciprocal responsibility of all
for all can be affirmed by as many as possible,
even though their reasons for the affirmation
will vary.[38]

Reciprocal Support

Whereas Henkin contends that "universal
acceptance and universal commitment" to the
idea of human rights ought to be "articulated in
specific agreed-upon terms," we have argued
that the recognition and realization in practice of human rights can better be achieved
by allowing room for a plurality of *particular*

moral vocabularies, including religious ones. Moreover, we have suggested that the most robust conceptions of human dignity—the richest ontologies of the human—are often rooted in what is "thickest," and thus most distinctive, about various traditions, rather than in what they share. There is therefore no reason in principle to suppose that the universality of the idea of human rights is incompatible with the particularity of religion. Indeed, affirming the relevant sort of universality seems to require a footing within the particularity of a determinate tradition of some kind (whether religious or nonreligious). This is the central claim of *situated universalism*.

Of course, much will depend on the nature of the tradition in question, and it would be absurd to claim that *religion* (without further clarification of what one means by the term) is necessarily amenable to the idea of human rights. "Religion," after all, means different things to different people, and much religious belief and practice is clearly antithetical to the idea of human rights. As a result, the task of articulating religious grounds for the idea of human rights must remain *theological* and constructive. Yet all who support the idea— whatever their specific reasons—would do well to encourage such efforts by those in other traditions, religious and nonreligious alike.

This sort of generosity of spirit will perhaps be easier to muster once it is appreciated that multiple justifications are compatible with a single moral truth and, thus, that the "ownership" of human rights by any one tradition is not at stake. If this is correct, it should come as good news to human rights advocates of all persuasions. For in our present age, the idea of human rights needs all the friends it can get.

5

Christianity and Human Rights: A Historical Perspective

Historical relations between Christianity and human rights are complex and much debated. On the one hand, Christian notions of dignity, equality, freedom, and justice played an important role in the development of contemporary conceptions of personhood and universal rights. On the other hand, the realization of these rights in practice has been severely impeded by the churches' insistence on doctrinal orthodoxy, their persecution of dissenters and non-Christians, and their complicity with unjust social and political arrangements. Although there is much of great historical importance to which it is impossible to do justice in the limited space available here, this chapter attempts to trace in broad strokes the shape of this history by highlighting both positive and negative developments vis-à-vis human rights in Christian thought and practice.

The Early Church

As the first Christians struggled to make sense of the events concerning Jesus—his life, his teaching, and the horrific and humiliating circumstances of his death—different and sometimes conflicting interpretations swiftly arose. Some, at least, of his followers were united in the belief that Jesus had a central role in the continuing purposes of the God of Israel. These early Christian communities began to understand Jesus as the resurrected one, or as a unique messianic prophet, and eventually to worship him as God.

No doubt, some Christian communities expected the breaking in of the kingdom of God with immediate political consequences, but what was to become the mainstream came increasingly to understand salvation as an eschatological gift of faith, continuing beyond physical death, through the resurrected Christ. The world of temporal affairs was held to be of only provisional significance, to be exchanged sooner or later for the kingdom of heaven, and communities that stressed the sociopolitical aspects of Jesus' message were increasingly written out of the narrative—a signal example of the marginalization that takes place in the development of all religious traditions.

A community based on minor cultural groups and facing hostility had little obvious incentive to consider human rights issues in the majority culture. More pressing was the need to plead for tolerance and protection for its small and vulnerable congregations. Notions of tolerance and claims to equality took different shapes in different communities. The main emphasis of the influential Pauline communities was not to assert rights, but rather to act in humility and *kenosis*. This could, of course, become a powerful catalyst for the mission to privilege the rights of others, especially when coupled with the concern for strangers that ran powerfully through Jesus' teaching and action. But this line of thinking would come to fruition only when Christians became major players within the Roman Empire. Seemingly paradoxically, however, Christianity's association with power would also hinder its ability to live up to these ethical and religious ideals.

There can be little doubt that the emphasis on the development of christological and Trinitarian doctrine with which theological students become familiar today accurately reflects the main trajectory of intellectual activity throughout much of the history of the church. It entailed the need for agreed doctrinal criteria and often led to harsh treatment of those who produced minority reports. The infamous dictum that "error has no rights" effectively hindered respect for diversity. As the churches gained political significance, it became possible for them to mobilize the state against dissent. The assertion of theological certainty, which the cultural paradigms of the church increasingly seemed to require, led to religious intolerance and persecution.

As the quest to clarify the christological mystery became ever more intense and politicized, formulations that seemed to emphasize most effectively the supreme significance of Jesus Christ in the understanding of God came to be preferred. But there was a price to be paid for excluding those who espoused alternative, but often equally faithful, perspectives. Christians were persecuted. Christians persecuted. Theological imperatives seemed to point in opposite directions. On the one hand, love was the cardinal virtue. On the other hand, truth was paramount, and those who were in untruth or persuaded others of untrue doctrines were destroying souls; for this, severe punishment was the divine command.

As far as dialogue with non-Christian conceptions of transcendence was concerned, an earlier view of at least an element of complementarity between Christian and Greco-Roman philosophical and theological values gave way to a consistent devaluing of anything that was not explicitly "Christian." Paradigmatic of this tension is the work of Augustine, who, despite an astonishing command of classical culture, came to repudiate many of its central values. Moreover, his fateful interpretation of Luke 14:23—*cogite intrare* ("compel them to enter")—lent support to the persecution of dissenters and non-Christians.

There were, of course, factors central to the early Christian tradition that could be mobilized to affirm human dignity and commend unconditional empathy and compassion. Christians constantly heard sermons on texts exhorting love—for example, on Matthew 5:43 ("love your enemies") and John 15:12 ("love one another, as I have loved you"). Among the Apostolic Fathers, altruism characterizes the Letter to Diognetus (especially chapter 7), and the tradition of altruism was well established in preaching and charitable action. Tertullian and Athenagoras defended liberty of conscience for Christians. Lactantius, in a much quoted passage, goes further and defends all freedom of religion: "Liberty has chosen to dwell in religion. For nothing is so much a matter of free will as religion, and no one can be required to worship what one does not choose to worship."[1] Beyond this there is evidence for a raft of concerns arising out of biblical exposition for what we would today regard as human rights issues—Gregory of Nyssa's (rather isolated but clear) condemnation of slavery; explicit concern for widows, the poor, and the sick; and the development of almsgiving.

But the perceived need for conformity functioned in practice to drown out these motifs. The development of less authoritarian ways of thinking in society in general would be necessary to lead the church to discover what it already had, but had largely buried. To do this, it had to learn to restrain some of the exclusive tendencies of monotheism and the rhetoric of intolerance.

The Middle Ages

During the Middle Ages, Christendom was characterized by the paradox of amazing variety in faith and practice in many local areas, of cultural pluralism and intercultural thinking, set against an enduring tendency to confuse unity with uniformity, and to seek to force Christianity into a doctrinal and ethical straitjacket.

Thomas Aquinas used the *imago Dei* metaphor extensively to show that human beings, in distinction from all other animals, are made in God's image and capable of knowing God.

Stress on the dignity of the person helped to create conditions for the possibility of the development of a human rights culture.[2] Brian Tierney writes:

> In the twelfth century a concern for the moral integrity of human personality led to the first stirrings of natural rights theories. An autonomous church asserted its own rights and limited the power of the state so that it never became truly absolute. Individual civic rights grew up within a context of communal institutions that were shaped in part by the growing law of the church. These points have broader implications. They suggest that Western rights theories did not have their origin either in early modern capitalism or in late medieval nominalism; rather they are rooted more deeply in the tradition of Christian humanism that has shaped much of our political culture.[3]

Medieval canon law defined the rights of clergy, ecclesiastical organizations, church councils, the laity, and the poor. Thinkers of the period tended to write not about human rights in the abstract, but about social issues from which rights questions arise, such as war. The development, building on Roman law, of just-war theory illustrates the sophisticated state of Christian moral theology during this period.

However, these theological insights were often overridden in practice by more potent sociopolitical considerations, and the demands of orthodoxy limited the space available for theological development. Heresy was associated with malice and mortal sin, and charges of moral turpitude in the form of sexual deviance were frequently cited in heresy proceedings. Even the reformist jurist Jean Gerson saw heretics as traitors not only to the church, but also to God. Nevertheless, it must be acknowledged that the Middle Ages encompassed a wide variety of culture, theory, and practice, and (contrary to popular opinion today) were very far from being the darkness before the Reformation's dawn.

Reformation and Rights

The Reformation, anticipated in part by aspects of the Renaissance, brought an appeal to individual judgment and Christian liberty, which was to stimulate discussion of toleration a century later. But this was hampered by a tendency to equate the voice of conscience with the voice of God, and therefore to breed a new authoritarianism.[4] Calvin's Geneva, for instance, was built on the *consensus fidelium*, according to which the individual in the Reformed polity was under divine obligation to obey the ruling presbyters, acting on behalf of the divinely elect community. Despite Luther's strongly christological emphasis on individual freedom and Calvin's proclamation of the absolute freedom of the sovereign God, toleration did not extend to critics of the covenant community.

In his classic studies of the sixteenth century, Roland Bainton locates the springs of intolerance not in wickedness per se but in theological conviction.[5] Conscience had no claims as such: a person "must *be* right in order to have rights."[6] And if error had no rights, the enforcers of orthodoxy—of whatever stripe—recognized few limits. As Bainton observes, "It is the saints who burn the saints."[7] Official statistics of recorded executions among marginalized groups within Christendom hardly reflect the mass of accumulated misery inflicted on people who did not conform to ecclesiastical norms.[8]

Christians and Others

Of course, other Christians were not the only ones who suffered under the tyrannical fervor of the "saints." Jews, Muslims, and non-European peoples also feature prominently among the victims of church history. Throughout much of this history, to be Christian was to be anti-Jewish. Jesus, of course, was a Jew, and Christianity was originally a sect within Judaism—one of many reform movements in the first century. However, as Christianity developed into a distinct tradition and acquired political significance as the official religion of the Roman Empire, it claimed to have replaced Judaism in salvation history. According to the logic of this supercessionistic theology, the continued existence of Judaism was a scandal to the church, which claimed to be the "New Israel." Jews in Europe were demonized as "Christ killers," marginalized in ghettoes, and subjected to persecution and periodic pogroms. During the Middle Ages, crusaders en route to Jerusalem slaughtered Jews in Europe. Nor was hostility to Jews limited to medieval Catholicism. In his later years, Luther famously argued that synagogues should be burned and that Jews should be turned out of their homes; deprived of rabbis, prayer books, and Talmuds; stripped of their belongings; and forced to work for Christians. Many Jews fled to Muslim lands, where they were usually treated with greater religious toleration, as "People of the Book."

But if Jews were reviled for their failure to embrace Christianity, Muslims were abhorred as heretics, and Islam was treated as a non-Trinitarian corruption of the true faith. In Dante's *Inferno*, for example, Muhammad and his son-in-law 'Ali are placed in hell, where they are depicted as being repeatedly mutilated by a devil as "disseminators of scandal and schism." Anti-Islamic sentiment culminated in the Crusades. Although Christian Europeans were unsuccessful in their repeated attempts to drive Muslims out of the Holy Land, they did manage to expel the Moors (Andalusian Muslims) and Jews from Spain in 1492, the same year Columbus made his famous voyage.

In 1453 Constantinople was captured by the Ottoman Turks, and—inspired by Columbus and other European explorers—Christians in Europe soon turned their attention westward. During the period of colonial expansion in the New World, Aristotle's notion that slaves are naturally in servitude and Aquinas's contention that slavery is a punishment for sin were used to justify the conquest and exploitation of indigenous peoples. However, a few theologians opposed these developments on theological grounds. During this period, Bartolome de las Casas emerged as a prophetic figure in the history of rights discussion. Las Casas invoked the legal maxim *quod omnes tangit debet ab omnibus approbari* ("what touches all should be approved by all") to call for government by consent. But although he was generous toward indigenous peoples, Las

Casas was harsh toward heretics; then as now, respect for difference was usually selective. It would ultimately take the Enlightenment to break the mold of authoritarian tradition and free up the many resources for affirming human dignity and individual rights that remained frozen in the sediment of the classical christological tradition.

Enlightenment and the Nineteenth Century

The liberal theology of the Enlightenment and the nineteenth century, with its emphasis on a humanist Christology "from below" and its concern for the social ethic of the kingdom of God, paved the way for later theological concern for the marginalized. The Christologies of Schleiermacher and Ritschl portrayed the man Jesus as a model of compassion and kindness, bringing a state of blessedness or reconciliation to the individual (in Schleiermacher's case) and exhorting communal social action toward the construction of the kingdom of God (in the case of Ritschl). These new Christologies resolved some of the problems of the authoritarian community but created others. However, the gains were much greater than the losses, since it is the critical rationality we owe to the period that makes possible the constantly changing modern critical research paradigm.

During this era, there were increasing theological pleas for tolerance and religious liberty. However, the Enlightenment is rightly criticized for its limited vision and authoritarian consequences. The negative effects resulted from the fact that Enlightenment notions of toleration, freedom, justice, and equality were limited to particular interest groups and did not go nearly far enough.

The nineteenth century witnessed fierce debates among Christians over slavery. As Mark Noll has shown, those who defended slavery often did so using scriptural proof texts, whereas those who opposed it on theological grounds generally appealed to Christian notions of equality and freedom.[9] Enslaved Christians found special meaning in biblical accounts of liberation, such as the story of the Exodus. Insofar as it involved a theological debate about scriptural interpretation, the dispute over slavery prefigured debates over gender and sexuality in the twentieth and twenty-first centuries.

The Twentieth Century

The great supporter of Christocentric theology in the twentieth century was, of course, Karl

Barth. To what extent may his Christology be seen as a Christology for human rights? On the positive side, Barth's theology of grace was a profound apprehension of the freedom of the gospel and the unconditional love of God at the center of creation. The human dignity of all persons, male and female, in the image of God is affirmed. All are equal in the sight of God, and social justice is important. In Christ, there is neither slave nor free. Political freedom is affirmed. Every sort of totalitarian political ideology is idolatry. Since Jesus Christ died to redeem all humanity, talk of capital punishment is tantamount to blasphemy. War is always sinful, and nonviolence is almost always the Christian option. Barth famously refused to take the oath of allegiance to Hitler and lost his academic appointment in 1935.

On the negative side, Barth demonstrates a much criticized adherence to patriarchal biblical patterns in relations between women and men, and it is hard to find explicit reference to civil rights, discrimination against ethnic minorities, or world poverty. There are few references to "human rights" as such in the *Church Dogmatics*. It has been suggested, in relation to "the Jewish question" in the 1930s, that Barth concentrated on looking at the issues theologically rather than politically and therefore failed to do justice to the horrors that were becoming a daily occurrence. In his thought, Judaism becomes Jewish history within the *Heilsgeschichte* (salvation history), and the political reality is masked. Barth was later to regret that there was no mention of Jewish persecution in the 1934 Barmen Declaration.

A deeper attention to the German political realities of the time and their implications for Jews is evidenced in the life and work of Dietrich Bonhoeffer. As a theologian and pastor, Bonhoeffer became increasingly alarmed by a regime that seemed to him to be taking the authority of God upon itself. His Christology led him to critique an ecclesiastical triumphalism that was unconcerned about those outside the church's own ranks. In the name of Christ, he protested the persecution of Jews and those who criticized the government. In this respect, Bonhoeffer was sadly the exception; although there were private protests, the historian Daniel Jonah Goldhagen notes, "Never once did any German bishop, Catholic or Protestant, speak out publicly on behalf of the Jews."[10] Though opposed to violence, Bonhoeffer became involved in a conspiracy to assassinate Hitler—an act he regarded as the lesser evil. When his role in the resistance was exposed, Bonhoeffer was imprisoned in a series of concentration camps and later executed.

Among leading European Catholic thinkers, Karl Rahner's anthropological approach to Christology led him to place a distinctive emphasis on human dignity. The consequences are rarely worked out in detail, but his theology has inspired many who continue to work on human rights issues from within the Catholic Church. Virtually the same may be said of Edward Schillebeeckx, for whom emphasis on present experience implies a high premium on human freedom.

However, it was largely outside academic theology that the influence of Christian conviction was to make a decisive difference to human rights culture in the twentieth century. In his book *For All Peoples and All Nations*, John Nurser demonstrates in detail how Christians such as Fred Nolde, now largely forgotten even by the churches, had a significant effect on the creation of the Universal Declaration of Human Rights.[11] The founding of the World Council of Churches (WCC) in 1938 gave rise to a continuous series of ecumenical committees and conferences with the aim "to write the peace," as John R. Mackay put it in 1942, and to avoid the mistakes of Versailles. A small group of ecumenical activists succeeded, with much support from Eleanor Roosevelt, in persuading the United Nations to adopt the Universal Declaration on December 10, 1948.

In the second half of the twentieth century, Christian input to human rights concerns continued, with varying degrees of effectiveness. This is most obviously seen in numerous denominational and congregational commissions for social justice and peace. The WCC continued to be engaged with human rights at various levels, from UN and government lobbying to supporting the work of NGOs. Through the Commission of the Churches on International Affairs, it contributes to the UN Human Rights Council. During the seventies and eighties, many churches became explicitly concerned with human rights, particularly in connection with environmentalism, global economic development, and the threat of nuclear war.

However, as these themes came to be seen as inextricably connected with geopolitics, perhaps tainted with secular associations, and often uncomfortably related to internal church tensions concerning power and authority, enthusiasm for human rights culture waned. Beginning in the 1970s, the WCC came under deep suspicion in conservative political and theological circles. Changes in theological fashion, together with an awareness of the problematic nature of a simple endorsement of the values of the West, led to a concentration on more internalized ecclesiology.

One important exception, as we saw in chapter 1, was constituted by the proliferation, often outside the European and North American theological guild, of emancipatory theologies. By focusing on those who have traditionally been marginalized—the poor, women, racial and ethnic minorities, the disabled, or the gay, lesbian, bisexual, and transgendered community—liberation theologians of varying stripes have helped to put human rights issues at the forefront of theological concern, even for theologians who pursue quite different methodologies.

The Bible and Its Interpretation

Where is the Bible in all this reflection? The christological tradition relating to justice and equity is firmly embedded in biblical interpretation, and there are numerous narrative episodes in both the Hebrew Bible and the New Testament that might give rise to reflection and practice in a human rights direction. However, there are also many biblical passages that militate strongly against human rights as we understand them today, including injunctions to genocide and numerous instances of cultural discrimination. These strands live on in the history of interpretation and may inhibit the apprehension of rights concepts.

We have already noted the influence of biblical notions of justice and righteousness in encouraging awareness of human rights. All are made equal and given identity in Christ, and this gift is made available to all humanity. Yet as many studies have shown, biblical imagery was often as much a factor in obstructing the development of humane attitudes (for example, in the cases of capital punishment, slavery, and patriarchy) as it was in facilitating it. Christological passages advocating unconditional love and forgiveness are not especially prominent in the history of biblical exegesis. The image of Christ as absolute monarch and implacable judge was at least as influential as that of Christ our fellow sufferer in identification with those at the point of greatest need.

In the New Testament, discussion of most theological issues is naturally brought to focus in relation to Jesus Christ. But the New Testament is built upon the Old, and the Hebrew Bible contains considerable material that is relevant to rights issues and of great significance for Christianity. That material is also, of course, of basic significance for Judaism, which has made considerable contributions to the development of modern rights theories and institutions. The Hebrew Bible is read by many rights theorists as providing a universal framework for moral law under God and a basis in respect for human well-being. In addition to its centrality within Jewish thought, this position is developed in Protestant theology by Max Stackhouse, in Catholic social thought by Michael Perry, and importantly by Muslim writers.

However, it must be acknowledged that the biblical corpus also includes a considerable body of "texts of terror," which have been used effectively to oppose most modern advances in human rights. Racism, slavery, the oppression of women and gays, anti-Semitism, and xenophobia—all have been vigorously supported on biblical grounds. "Literalist" interpretations have been strengthened by reading the Bible through the lens of unexamined cultural assumptions. But the texts themselves, embedded in their particular cultures, have been a prime source of opposition to human rights and therefore of oppression for millions of people through the ages.

This material can be regarded as evidence of the earthen vessels in which the biblical treasure is contained—not a mystery to be accepted and somehow included in the Christian agenda, but rather an obstacle to be overcome in the developing tradition of research and interpretation. But Christians who believe, as many millions do, in the Bible as the literal, inspired word of God have great difficulty negotiating the hard texts of biblical prohibitions and injunctions. Those who wish to take these texts seriously while also considering more progressive alternatives must turn to other sources of theological insight. In fact, many conservative Christians have come around to doing this, on issues ranging from slavery (in the nineteenth century) to the status of women (in the twentieth). However, there is no single automatic line of development here, and in many instances, the more literal stance is reinforced. In fact, there is evidence that, contrary to the expectations of nineteenth- and twentieth-century scholars, fundamentalist modes of interpretation are sharply on the rise today. This implies a continuing need for dialogue, advocacy, and persuasion on the part of progressive Christians.

The Need for Discernment

The foregoing survey, though brief and necessarily far from comprehensive, suggests that the history of Christianity with respect to human rights is at best ambiguous. Christians today are the inheritors of a legacy from which there is much to be retrieved and much else to be discarded. The task of heirs is to discern which is which—to repent from evil and to cling to what is good.

Reflecting on these historical developments, it would appear that the proliferation of notions of religious tolerance and respect was among the most important steps toward the growth of a culture of human rights. As long as people were convinced that there was a single God-given way of thinking and acting, and that this was the possession of their own particular group, there was little chance for real progress. Despite an enormous history of christological reflection, the notion of a Christ who is the instantiation of vulnerable, self-giving love was often eclipsed by imagery of Christ the judge, who approves orthodoxy and consigns the errant to damnation. What sort of Christian theology might hope to avoid some of the pitfalls of the past and contribute to a future in which the ideal of human rights is more fully realized in practice? This question is the topic of the next, and final, chapter.

6

Toward a Theology
of Human Rights

This chapter examines some aspects of the relationship between Christian theology—specifically, Christology—and human rights. To be sure, we cannot impose theological categories on rights dialogue if it is to remain genuine dialogue. But what can be said is that Christian communities and individuals have drawn strength from their faith that at the root of all existence is a power that is entirely noncoercive, and that that power is the power of unconditional love. Christian faith affirms that human beings are the field in which God has become incarnate in the shape of self-dispossessing love.

As we saw earlier, human rights discourse is premised upon the affirmation of universal human dignity. But to affirm human dignity is not necessarily to affirm human goodness.

Indeed, it is generally necessary to affirm the former precisely because of the evil and violence of which human beings are capable. Thus, any anthropology consistent with the idea of human rights, whether theological or otherwise, must strike a balance between an overly positive view of human nature and an overly negative one. Christology—at its most inclusive, reflection on the self-giving character of God's love in the world—serves as the linchpin between Christian theology and Christian anthropology, between a doctrine of God and an account of human nature in both its frailty and its dignity. As such, it is an ideal site on which to develop a distinctively Christian ontology of the human—an account of human dignity rooted in the love of God. In Christ, it can be affirmed, God invests human life with dignity precisely by sharing in the suffering that human beings inflict on one another.

Of course, the eschatological element of faith, its openness to the future, serves as a reminder that all our theories are only pointers in the direction of the mystery of the divine love. The sociohistorical dimension of faith, with its uncertainties and its cultural and temporal limitations, constitutes the other side of this theory of truth. We do indeed participate in the life of God, but as pilgrims on the way to a mystery. That distinctively Christian tradition centered on the self-abandonment of God does not claim a monopoly on either visions of the common good or construals of God. The Christian vision articulated here is thus offered as a contribution, along with other contributions, both religious and non-religious, to the practical tasks of delivering human rights solutions at points of greatest urgency.

God Instantiated

It seems clear that some Christologies have his-torically been entirely inadequate to articulate faithfully the character of God's self-dispossessing love, precisely because they have obscured the thrust of the gospel toward that concern for the marginalized in society that was central to the life of Jesus. Here liberation and emancipatory theologies have performed a crucial service of retrieval, and "non-absolutist" Christologies have pointed the way to a conceptually more open approach. At the same time, however, Christian faith has classically drawn strength from an understanding of Jesus Christ as effective not only through his life but also through his death, which has been seen as making a distinctive difference in the nature of the universe as God's creation, and through his resurrection as the first transformative product of that difference. This is why faith is quintessentially a trust in God against the appearance of things, and Christians are often prepared to think and act *contra mundum*.

A Christology for human rights pays particular attention to the many dimensions of the continuing power of reconciliation in Christ. In the events concerning Jesus, we see God's instantiation in a specific human being, identified with the denial of all human rights, without remainder. But victimization is not the final word. By participating in human suffering, God subverts the forces of violence through love. This cluster of events can be envisaged through different theological categories, notably of incarnation and inspiration, each of which makes its own contribution to conceiving the mystery.

Incarnation, which itself may be conceived in different and sometimes overlapping ways, points to the reality of the involvement of God with human bodies. What happens to bodies is important to God, who—according to Christian faith—has shared human embodiment in every range of experience. In this distinctively Christian ontology of the human, we find the resources for a universal conception of human dignity: human beings participate in God's image, because God participates in humanity as a victim of human rights abuse.[1] Although the Christ event has often been read as an affirmation of God as the real locus of value, it suggests equally that God's goal is fulfilled in the flourishing of human person-hood. Incarnation is God's affirmation of the value, in the perspective of God's love, of every human being. It simultaneously has a wider connotation, for it is a catalyst for the reconciliation of the whole created order.

The consequences of incarnation include the creation of visible communities of Christian faith, which continue in communion with God through word and sacrament, response to proclamation and participation in Eucharist, in the tradition of the gospel. Where the church is outward-facing as well as inward-facing, there is a constructive relationship between incarnation and response, but where the church is purely inward-facing, this relationship is diminished.

Further dimensions of the archetypal divine instantiation are expressed by inspiration. The consequence of resurrection is the presence within the created order of the spirit of the risen Christ. Spirit is not in conflict with, but complements, embodiment. Within Christian community, the spirit is always related to the focal areas of word and sacrament. Precisely how these are related has been the subject of endless sacramental controversy. What matters here are the intrinsic connection and the central importance of both.

Two thousand years of Christianity have shown that the spirit of Christlikeness is nevertheless not confined to Christian community. Christians have experienced divine love as active in other religions, as well as in secular spheres, in individual lives, in social and political developments, sometimes from within the church and sometimes challenging the churches from outside. Wherever human agency produces outcomes in love and compassion, Christians may give thanks for Christomorphic traces of divine action, the spirit of Christlikeness in the created order. This is the salvific outcome of the dynamic sequence of the life, death, and resurrection of Jesus Christ.

There is then a basic bond between the humiliated and exalted Christ and attention to human rights in all its dimensions. Christian theology will understand action for human rights not as identical with, but certainly as caught up within, the much wider and more mysterious dynamic of the cosmic presence of the divine love. Because faith claims this underlying ground, it benefits from immersion in an inexhaustible vision, however unpromising the current outlook in any given area may become.

Inclusive Partnership

But faith is always vulnerable to forms of triumphalism. We cannot say of ourselves that, because we are trying to respond in loving action to our understanding of the divine love, we are necessarily agents of divine action. This way madness lies. We have seen only too plainly the disastrous consequences of Christian self-delusion and abuse of power in the past and in the present. In this light, we can say only that we are hoping, in a provisional way and to the best of our ability, to follow in the way of Christian discipleship. But we may hope also to recognize in the actions of others the manifestation of the divine love and regard this as a huge encouragement for the future of God's purposes of love, peace, and justice.

As we saw in the previous chapter, the history of Christian thought and action is a history that calls for humility: how could we have gotten so much so wrong so often? Yet there are still outbursts of transparent goodness produced by the Christian gospel and shared with a wider humanity. These are what faith has understood as the "fruits of the spirit." Progress here will involve a comprehensive renunciation of traditions of cultural and religious superiority. On the one hand, it is important to distinguish Christian contributions from the Western or neocolonial packaging in which they have so often been offered. But equally, on the other hand, the real value of Western Christian thinking and action to the human future need not be disparaged or underplayed. Despite its serious flaws and its only partial perspective, the Christian tradition is also a hugely valuable legacy upon which to build in partnership with others.

On some occasions, it will be desirable to offer an explicitly Christian approach to justice and rights. But on other occasions, these grounds will remain entirely implicit. This is not a matter of deviousness or hesitation. Loving action in society often takes place anonymously and is all the more effective for this anonymity.

An Enduring Vision

A christological perspective has both positive and negative value in contributing to human rights issues. Positively, reflection on Christ has encouraged Christians to work by themselves and with others in effectively addressing many areas of human rights concern: individual liberty, torture, justice, and hunger. However, it has largely been ineffective where scriptural tradition has had a strong influence in inhibiting rights—most notably in the areas of gender and sexuality. Here perhaps we have to look elsewhere for guidance.

But Christianity has historically exhibited a capacity for change and development (for example, in relation to such issues as slavery and race), and we should not expect that today's status quo will remain the norm a hundred years from now. The Christian tradition has potential, in reflecting on the dynamic of relationality and respect for others expressed in the events concerning Jesus Christ, to make significant contributions, even in areas where it has largely failed in the past. By critically facing up to its failures in a spirit of genuine repentance, it may even play a future role in encouraging other traditions, religious and secular, to confront their weaknesses and make appropriate changes of attitude and action. As Donald Shriver aptly reminds us, "We are all vulnerable to collaboration in the doing of great evil to our neighbors: If Christians bring any gifts to politics, this truth about us ought to be one of them."[2] Christianity may also learn from such dialogue to widen its own base of human rights commitments in the future. It can remain open to respond to the christological vision by working with organizations outside the church in areas where this is likely to be effective. In this way, human rights action may be seen as one of the consequences of the form of Christ in the world.

A Framework for Persistence

A Christian contribution to human rights action—specifically, a contribution based on reflection upon Christ—can be offered on several different levels. First, there is the level of *relationality*. Jesus the Christ is who he is and does what he does through his being as *being-through-relationality*. Often, a Christian commitment to embody the virtues of relationality is most sorely tested within the context of the church itself. We have to recognize that different Christians will have different views of current flashpoints and different priorities. Where there are deep differences, we have to struggle to maintain mutual respect and communication without sacrificing those on the margins. It is worth remembering that Christians who are deeply critical of one group of marginalized people may be hugely supportive of other groups. We cannot afford to waste resources on unnecessary internecine quarrels that weaken the church's ability to respond to those in need. There is reason to hope that separate support of different abused groups may lead in time to awareness of common grounds for affirmation and respect.

Second, we must respond in *solidarity* with others by privileging groups whose human rights are threatened. Christ is crucified outside the gate, outside the magic circle. Everyone feels marginalized in some ways at different times. Making the imaginative leap into looking at issues from this perspective is both possible and necessary. Not all marginalization amounts to denial of human rights, but denial is often the next step. It is incumbent on all Christians to do what they can to act in solidarity with those most in need. Whether solidarity is achieved by secret diplomacy or vocal public advocacy (or a combination of both) will depend on what is likely to be most effective in specific cases.

Third, it must be remembered that both *insiders and outsiders* have valuable experiences and insights, and that these resources are most effective when pooled. One of the most important needs for those who are oppressed (by torture, hunger, racism, and so on) is to retain a sense of self-respect in the face of general vilification. This requires the combined efforts of Christians both inside and outside the issue. For instance, only women perhaps can fully understand the devastating effects of patriarchal attitudes and practices in church and society over the past two thousand years, but men can take the trouble to immerse themselves in the issues and begin to dismantle the barriers that they have themselves erected or maintained.

Reconciliation and Forgiveness

We have characterized the Christ of faith as the icon of the self-giving, outward-facing love of God. In human relationships, individual and social, this translates into a catalytic capacity for reconciliation. Reconciliation recognizes damaged relationships, which are intrinsic to human rights violations, and facilitates restoration, restitution, and forgiveness. Reconciliation cannot be imposed from above, and its shape cannot be determined unilaterally. It requires patient preparation of the ground, as well as acknowledgment of fault. As Archbishop Desmond Tutu notes in *No Future without Forgiveness*, "Forgiving and being reconciled are not about pretending that things are other than they are."[3] A Christian understanding of reconciliation will not necessarily always require an overtly "Christian" outcome. It can be understood as *human* reconciliation, worked at through faith in Christ and reflecting the divine love.

Forgiveness is not in the first instance the appropriate framework for those who have been the deniers of rights. Imagined transgressions on the part of the discriminated against have to be recognized as arising from the pressures of the situation in which they have been placed, and a new basis of equal partnership must be created. Yet here, too, there can be a significant role for reconciliation. The struggle for rights can produce victims, often unintended, on both sides. Few countries have shown such an amazing example of this capacity for reconciliation and forgiveness in the wake of widespread and institutionalized injustice as South Africa.

Reconciliation is not something that occurs spontaneously or instantaneously in complex conflicts; it requires action at various levels, from the general to the minutely particular, and calls for a cumulative strategy that is neither distracted by detail nor marooned in romantic generality. The language of forgiveness and reconciliation can be manipulated. Yet an awareness of forgiveness linked to compassion is a hugely valuable Christian contribution to the complex negotiation of the fruits of human rights in society. Forgiveness

has often opened up the dimension of generosity, as a catalyst to move otherwise intrac-
table issues forward.

Christology for Human Rights

This chapter has attempted to sketch the out-
lines of a Christology consistent with the
idea and claims of universal human rights—a
Christology *for* human rights. But human
rights do not exhaust the contents of Christian theology. Here it is important to remember that human-rights thinking is minimalistic
by design, representing a floor rather than a
ceiling for moral endeavor. A world in which
human rights were realized in practice would
not of itself constitute the kingdom of God,
though arguably it would be a good deal
closer to that ideal than the world in which
we currently live.

Christians believe that Jesus Christ plays
an indispensable and decisive role in God's
purpose for humanity. However, there is no
consensus on the nature of Christ's significance. The apprehension of the central struc-
turing elements of faith is affected by local
theological cultures and concepts, as well as
by the political and social contexts in which
theology is done and which it aims in turn to
illuminate. A multiplicity of interpretations is

thus wholly appropriate and attests to the richness of meaning implicit in the Christian tradition. If these Christologies are to contribute to the global struggle for human dignity, they should encapsulate the nature of the Christian understanding of the love of God, illuminating the self-giving, self-dispossessing nature of divine reality as a pattern for human relationships. Within these broad boundaries, individual people and communities should be free to contribute in their own ways, and no *single* approach should be understood as *the* authorized way.

It may not be desirable to build all houses in a cruciform shape, as a sub-Barthian view of Christ and culture might suggest. But it is possible to build communities in ways that enhance humanity and the possibility of exercising human capabilities, in ways that are consonant with the promise of Jesus Christ to bring life more abundant, life that is fair and just.

Postscript: An Invitation to the Struggle

The claims of human rights make demands on all of us, and the realization of such rights in practice will require the development and maintenance of a "culture of human rights." These are tasks to which each of us can contribute, no matter our location, circumstances, or background. Opportunities are many; the challenge is to make the demanding move from spectator to participant in the global struggle for human dignity. By way of conclusion, we offer the following ten suggestions for effective action:

1. Think globally. Ours is an increasingly interconnected world; what happens in one part of it affects people in other parts. Get informed: educate yourself about what is going on in other countries, as well as in your own. The denial of human rights anywhere is a scandal everywhere.

2. Act locally. Start where you are, as this is where you are likely to be most effective. Ask tough questions. What impact do the choices made by elected officials in your country (and ultimately by you as a voter) have in other (perhaps poorer) countries? How do you spend and invest your money? Where do your food and clothes come from?

3. Try to avoid the arrogance of cultural or national imperialism. Human rights advocacy is often most effective and its results most enduring when it is initiated from within the culture in question. Efforts by outsiders to effect cultural change, however well meaning, are seldom as well received.

4. Work in partnership with others. Remember that you are not alone. Apart from the necessary political and diplomatic activity of governments, much human rights work continues to be achieved through the efforts of humanitarian organizations and advocacy networks. Join (or start) a human rights group on your campus, at your church, or in your neighborhood. Help raise awareness about human rights issues within your community.

5. Have faith that human rights action does make a difference. Faith in the efficacy of human rights action can also entail *keeping faith* with the traditions in which we stand—

recognizing their potential for affirming universal human dignity, even as we acknowledge and attempt to address their many inadequacies. For Christians, moreover, faith in human rights can be rooted in faith in God's self-giving love for humanity.

6. Keep hope alive. When we are faced with great suffering and horrendous evils, it is tempting to succumb to resignation, cynicism, and despair. Take courage from the example of others, and cultivate the virtue of hope (as distinct from naive optimism).

7. Practice peace and reconciliation. Don't become embittered by the world's evils. Support those who are victimized, but don't demonize oppressors or confuse vengeance with justice.

8. Make the most of the available resources, including the moral and intellectual resources of your (religious) tradition.

9. Persevere. Projects without adequate planning, resources, and willpower almost inevitable fail and may leave the problems they were meant to address in a much worse state than before. This applies to large-scale political interventions and small-scale endeavors alike.

10. Focus on what matters most. Don't become so preoccupied with any particular goal, strategy, or theory that you neglect the needs of the individuals it is meant to benefit.

Notes

Introduction

1. "Desmond Tutu on God, Bush and the Tsunamis," Newsweek Web Exclusive, 30 December 2004, http://www.msnbc.msn.com/id/6769668/site/newsweek/ (27 April 2007).

2. Desmond M. Tutu, "Preface," *Religious Human Rights in Global Perspective: Religious Perspectives*, ed. John Witte Jr. and Johan D. van der Vyver (The Hague: Martinus Nijhoff, 1996), xvi.

3. See, for example, Elizabeth Isichei, *A History of Christianity in Africa* (Grand Rapids: Eerdmans, 1995), 306. The Dutch Reformed Church in South Africa was often called "the National Party at prayer." Indeed, as Lyn S. Graybill notes, "Dutch Reformed churchmen have boasted that it was their church, and not the National Party, that first laid down the principles and framework of apartheid." Lyn S. Graybill, *Religion and Resistance Politics in South Africa* (Westport, Conn.: Praeger, 1995), 2.

4. Thus, in the same interview in which he compared religion to a knife, Tutu suggested that "religion in and of itself is morally neutral."

5. Michael J. Perry, *The Idea of Human Rights: Four Inquiries* (New York: Oxford University Press, 1998), 13.

6. See Michael Ignatieff, "Human Rights as Idolatry," in *The Tanner Lectures on Human Values* 22 (Salt Lake City: University of Utah Press, 2001), 300, 320. In contrast to the approach we advocate, Ignatieff defends the idea of human rights in prudential terms, rather than by appeal to religious or philosophical foundations. He borrows the phrase "secular religion" from

Elie Wiesel, "A Tribute to Human Rights," in *The Universal Declaration of Human Rights: Fifty Years and Beyond*, ed. Y. Danieli et al. (Amityville, N.Y.: Baywood, 1999), 3.

7. Latin American church leaders did not always take the side of the oppressed, and some played the role of oppressors. In October 2007, Father Christian Federico von Wernich, an Argentine priest, was sentenced to life in prison for crimes against humanity. The first Roman Catholic priest to be convicted of human rights abuses committed during the recent period of dictatorship in Latin America, von Wernich served as a police chaplain and informant for the 1976–1983 military government in Argentina. "In testimony, von Wernich was alleged to have been present during at least three murders, at one point washing blood off his hands with the executioners. He called the killings a 'patriotic act' performed 'in the name of God,' according to sworn statements." Patrick J. McDonnell, "Priest's Conviction Awakens Old Ghosts," *Los Angeles Times*, October 21, 2007: A7.

1. Human Rights and Christian Witness: A Case Study

1. "Murder at the Altar," *Time*, 7 April 1980.

2. Oscar Romero, *La Voz de Los Sin Voz: La Palabra Viva de Monseñor Romero*, ed. R. Cardenal, I. Martín-Baró, and J. Sobrino (San Salvador: UCA Editores, 1980), 291 (author's translation).

3. Indeed, through a series of rebroadcasts, Romero's sermons could be heard throughout Latin America.

4. Romero, *La Voz de Los Sin Voz*, 291.

5. Ibid., 280.

6. Ibid., 292.

7. Marie Dennis, Renny Golden, and Scott Wright, *Oscar Romero: Reflections on His Life and Writings* (Maryknoll, N.Y.: Orbis, 2000), 9.

8. Security forces killed 514 people in March 1980 alone. "Many of the murders bore evidence of systematic planning such as the hunting down of teachers. They were being murdered on a systematic basis, averaging one every three days." Ignacio Martín-Baró, "Oscar Romero: Voice of the Downtrodden," in Oscar Romero, *Voice of the Voiceless: The Four Pastoral Letters and Other Statements*, trans. Michael J. Walsh (Maryknoll, N.Y.: Orbis, 1990), 17. Martín-Baró was himself killed in 1989 along with five other Jesuit professors, their housekeeper, and her daughter by soldiers from the U.S.-trained Atlacatl Battalion, acting on orders from the director of El Salvador's Military College.

9. Dennis et al., *Oscar Romero*, 10–11.

10. Jon Sobrino, *Archbishop Romero: Memories and Reflections*, trans. Robert R. Barr (Maryknoll, N.Y.: Orbis, 1999), 9–10.

11. Ibid., 9. "Conversion" may be too strong a term, given that Romero was never wholly insensitive to the concerns of the poor. However, it is clear that Grande's death marked a turning point for Romero and precipitated a new self-awareness of the prophetic vocation that would define his later years. Sobrino writes, "I believe that this phenomenon can be called a conversion—not so much in the sense of ceasing to do evil and beginning to do good but in the sense of grasping the will of God and being able to implement it, and this in the spirit of deep, radical change." Ibid., 8.

12. Ibid., 16.

13. Ibid., 10.

14. See Roberto Cuéllar, "Monseñor Oscar Romero: Human Rights Apostle," in *Monsignor Romero: A Bishop for the Third Millennium*, ed. Robert S. Pelton (Notre Dame: University of Notre Dame Press, 2004), 35–46.

15. Ibid., 38.

16. Romero, *La Voz de Los Sin Voz*, 294. Readers interested in Romero's own words should also consult Romero, *Voice of the Voiceless* (an English translation of some of the material from *La Voz de Los Sin Voz*); Oscar Romero, *A Shepherd's Diary*, trans. Irene B. Hodgson (Cincinnati: St. Anthony Messenger Press, 1993) (a diary he kept from March 31, 1978, to March 20, 1980); and Oscar Romero, *The Violence of Love*, compiled and trans. James R. Brockman (Farmington, Pa.: Plough, 1988) (a collection of quotations).

17. John Langan, "The Individual and the Collectivity in Christianity," in *Religious Diversity and Human Rights*, ed. Irene Bloom, J. Paul Martin, and Wayne L. Proudfoot (New York: Columbia University Press, 1996), 172.

18. Ibid., 154–55.

19. Ibid., 171.

20. Daniel H. Levine and Scott Mainwaring, "Religion and Popular Protest in Latin America: Contrasting Experiences," in *Power and Popular Protest: Latin American Social Movements*, ed. Susan Eckstein (Berkeley: University of California Press, 1989), 211. Romero alludes to these repressive conditions in his Third Pastoral Letter: "The first conclusion of any impartial analysis of the right of association must be that groups in agreement with the government or protected by it have complete freedom. Organizations, on the other hand, that voice dissent from the

government—political parties, trade unions, rural organizations—find themselves hindered or even prevented from exercising their right to organize legally." Romero, *Voice of the Voiceless*, 90.

21. Interestingly, Levine and Mainwaring found that CEBs that were started for overtly political purposes were less politically effective that those with more "religious" goals. See Levine and Mainwaring, "Religion and Popular Protest," 212.

22. Romero, *Voice of the Voiceless*, 96.

23. Ibid., 184.

24. For a detailed account of these developments see Harvey Cox, *The Silencing of Leonardo Boff: The Vatican and the Future of World Christianity* (Oak Park, Ill.: Meyer-Stone, 1988).

25. Interestingly, prior to his "conversion" in 1977, Romero himself criticized the christologies being developed at the time by Sobrino and other Latin American theologians, once going as far as to characterize them as "rationalistic, revolutionary, [and] hate-filled." His views eventually changed, and he apologized for some of his earlier remarks. See Sobrino, *Archbishop Romero*, 4–6.

26. Jon Sobrino, Preface, in *Systematic Theology: Perspectives from Liberation Theology*, ed. Jon Sobrino and Ignacio Ellacuría (Maryknoll, N.Y.: Orbis, 1996), ix.

27. We are grateful to Dean Brackley, S.J., of the University of Central America "José Simeón Cañas" for providing poverty estimates.

2. What Are Human Rights?

1. Rex Martin and James W. Nickel have argued that although not all rights entail second-party duties, "any genuine right must involve some normative direction of the behavior of persons other than the holder." "Recent Work on the Concept of Rights," *American Philosophical Quarterly* 17:3 (July 1980): 167. It is simply in this broad sense that we employ the term *obligations* here.

2. As we shall see, however, it is also possible to speak of "group rights."

3. John Finnis, *Natural Law and Natural Rights* (Oxford: Oxford University Press, 1980), 205.

4. It might be argued that not all human rights entail obligations for every human being: some entail obligations only for a certain subset of human beings, such as those in one's government. Similarly, it might be argued, not every putative human right is a right belonging to all human beings. Some rights benefit only certain human beings, such as those living in

poverty, or women, or children. But to speak of these as *human* rights is simply another way of saying that these are rights to which every human being is entitled *in certain circumstances*, namely, the circumstance of being poor, or of being a woman, or of being a child. The same basic point can be made about obligations as well: human rights that limit what the government can do to you entail obligations with which all human beings must comply, provided that they find themselves in the right circumstances—provided, namely, that they are members of one's government. See Perry, *The Idea of Human Rights*, 47.

5. Brian Tierney argues that the language of rights emerged in canon law around 1150. Others have claimed to detect it even earlier. See, for example, Brian Tierney, *The Idea of Natural Rights* (Atlanta: Scholars Press, 1997); and Fred D. Miller, *Nature, Justice, and Rights in Aristotle's Politics* (Oxford: Oxford University Press, 1995). As Jeffrey Stout points out, however, the use of the term *rights* has evolved and is no longer restricted to role-specific statuses in the way it once was. See Jeffrey Stout, *Democracy and Tradition* (Princeton: Princeton University Press, 2004), 204–5.

6. Jack Donnelly, "Human Rights and Human Dignity: An Analytic Critique of Non-Western Conceptions of Human Rights," *American Political Science Review* 76:2 (June 1982): 312.

7. Annette C. Baier, *Moral Prejudices* (Cambridge, Mass.: Harvard University Press, 1994), 225–26.

8. Although human rights theory gives the individual a certain moral priority, thereby enabling criticism of the community, it need not adopt a conception of the self as atomistic or antecedently individuated. In the best human rights theory, the individual is conceived as being socially embedded and shaped. We are indebted to Sumner B. Twiss for emphasizing this point.

9. The Convention on the Prevention and Punishment of the Crime of Genocide had been adopted a day earlier, on December 9, 1948. It came into force in 1951, although the United States did not sign on to the treaty until 1988.

10. This is a reference to a famous speech that Franklin D. Roosevelt gave in 1941, in which he proclaimed that people have four basic freedoms: freedom of speech, freedom of religion, freedom from fear, and freedom from want. Eleanor Roosevelt was the head of the UN Commission on Human Rights, which drafted the declaration.

11. The United States signed the ICESCR in 1977 but did not ratify it. (Signing signals a state's satisfaction with the text of a treaty, whereas ratification—usually a second stage in the

process—signifies a state's willingness to be bound by that text. In the United States, it is the president who signs, whereas the Senate must consent for ratification.) The United States and China are the only members of the Security Council that have not ratified the treaty. Britain ratified both in 1976.

12. Of course, institutions of various kinds are required for the realization of all rights, including first-generation rights.

13. This feature is a source of controversy. How, it might be wondered, can an abstract entity like a "group" have rights? Carol C. Gould suggests a solution when she argues that group rights "pertain to groups as constituted entities and thus are rights derived from the rights of the constituent individuals who are members of the group and who have these group rights insofar as they are members of the group and not apart from these relations to each other." Carol C. Gould, *Globalizing Democracy and Human Rights* (New York: Cambridge University Press, 2004), 124.

14. However, the concept of rights is not the only—nor, it might be argued, always the most appropriate—moral category for addressing such challenges. If, for instance, rights do not exist without rights holders, then the consequences of damaging environmental policies on future generations (generations yet to be born) might better be addressed in a different idiom. Even so, some theorists argue that it can make sense to speak of the "rights" of "future persons." See, for example, Jeffrey Reiman, "Being Fair to Future People: The Non-Identity Problem in the Original Position," *Philosophy and Public Affairs* 35:1 (2007): 59–92.

15. David Beetham, "Human Rights as a Model for Cosmopolitan Democracy," in *Re-Imagining Political Community: Studies in Cosmopolitan Democracy*, ed. Daniele Archibugi, David Held, and Martin Köhler (Stanford, Calif.: Stanford University Press, 1998), 58.

16. The council was created in 2006 to replace the earlier Human Rights Commission, which had been criticized for excessive politicization.

17. The Bush administration requested that other states sign "impunity agreements" requiring them not to surrender to the ICC U.S. citizens accused of crimes within the scope of the court's jurisdiction.

18. Alasdair MacIntyre, *After Virtue*, 2nd ed. (Notre Dame, Ind.: University of Notre Dame Press, 1984), 67.

19. Ibid., 70, 69.

20. If that still seems strange, try substituting "quarks" in place of "rights."

3. Human Rights and the Problem of Grounding

1. Abdullahi A. An-Na'im, "The Synergy and Interdependence of Human Rights, Religion, and Secularism," in *Human Rights and Responsibilities in the World Religions*, ed. Joseph Runzo, Nancy M. Martin, and Arvind Sharma (Oxford: Oneworld, 2003), 28.

2. MacIntyre, *After Virtue*, 67.

3. Ludwig Wittgenstein, *Philosophical Investigations*, trans. G. E. M. Anscome (Englewood Cliffs, N.J.: Prentice Hall, 1958), 2:178.

4. One might in fact worry that such slogans erode the force of the claims on which they are parasitic. Something along these lines is clearly evident in the way terms like *fascist* and *Nazi* have come to be used as otherwise unremarkable political epithets.

5. It is important to note that human beings are in fact moved by the sight of (nonhuman) animals in pain. Of course, our reactions to animals and their suffering vary: consider our respective "attitudes" toward chimpanzees, dogs, cows, and cockroaches, as these are exhibited in our lives.

6. Ronald Dworkin, *Life's Dominion: An Argument about Abortion, Euthanasia, and Individual Freedom* (New York: Vintage, 1994), 84.

7. *Sacredness*, for Dworkin, is not an exclusively religious concept. It refers to dignity or non-instrumental value.

8. Perry, *The Idea of Human Rights*, 27.

9. Ibid., 28.

10. Charles Taylor, *Sources of the Self: The Making of the Modern Identity* (Cambridge, Mass.: Harvard University Press, 1989), 4.

11. Ibid., 5.

12. Ibid., 7.

13. Ibid., 5.

14. Ibid., 6.

15. Ibid.

16. Ibid., 8.

17. Ibid.

18. Unlike in the modern sciences, which prize dispassionate objectivity, ethical reflection demands attention to one's instincts. To prescind from these makes one less, not more, rational. It would be akin to attempting to do science without relying on one's senses.

19. Taylor, *Sources of the Self*, 9.

20. Robert Brandom notes, "Making something explicit is *saying* it: putting it into a form in which it can be given as a reason, and reasons demanded for it." Robert B. Brandom,

Making It Explicit: Reasoning, Representing, and Discursive Commitment (Cambridge, Mass.: Harvard University Press, 1994), xviii.

21. John Rawls, *A Theory of Justice* (Cambridge, Mass.: Belknap, 1971), 20. He writes, "It is an equilibrium because at last our principles and judgments coincide; and it is reflective since we know to what principles our judgments conform and the premises of their derivation." Ibid., 20.

22. Taylor, *Sources of the Self*, 5.

23. Perry, *The Idea of Human Rights*, 11.

24. The distinction between religion and nonreligion is, of course, fuzzy at best. Perry equates religion with a view of life according to which "the world is ultimately meaningful (in a way hospitable to our deepest yearnings)." Ibid., 16. However, this definition is surely broader than many self-described "nonreligious" people would be willing to grant.

25. Stout, *Democracy and Tradition*, 241.

26. Stout writes, "Natural-law and divine-command theories become mystifications when they assume that an ideal system or its axioms can function—or is already functioning—as *our criterion* for deciding which moral claims are true." Ibid., 245.

4. Universal Human Rights and Religious Particularity

1. Louis Henkin, "Religion, Religions, and Human Rights," *Journal of Religious Ethics* 26 (1998): 238.

2. Ibid., 238.

3. Ibid., 233–4.

4. Ibid., 238.

5. Louis Henkin, "Human Rights: Religious or Enlightened?" in *Religion and Human Rights: Competing Claims?* ed. Carrie Gustafson and Peter Juviler (Armonk, N.Y.: Sharpe, 1999), 34.

6. Constructivism can thus be categorized as an "epistemic," rather than a "realist," conception of moral truth.

7. This is the standard view put forward by, for example, Jürgen Habermas. A weaker version of constructivism would relax the stipulation that a valid norm must be acceptable to all *in light of the same interests*, thus making room for a plurality of distinct justifications, including (perhaps) religious ones. We are grateful to Abdullahi Ahmed An-Na'im for pointing this out in his comments on an earlier draft.

8. Note that universality in this first sense is a function largely of the command's syntax rather than its semantics: that

is, the implied object remains universal even if the word *murder* (or something similar) is substituted for *kill*.

9. See Richard Amesbury, *Morality and Social Criticism: The Force of Reasons in Discursive Practice* (Basingstoke, UK: Palgrave Macmillan, 2005).

10. For instance, Habermas defends a constructivist account of morality while otherwise maintaining a realist (that is, objectivist) view of (theoretical) truth: "A constructivist conception of the moral 'ought' does require an epistemic understanding of normative rightness. But if we want to do justice to realist intuitions, the concept of propositional truth must not be assimilated to this sense of rational acceptability under approximately ideal conditions." Jürgen Habermas, *Truth and Justification*, ed. and trans. Barbara Fultner (Cambridge, Mass.: MIT Press, 2003), 8.

11. Adopting realism about truth and/or moral objectivism need not commit one to a Platonistic conception of "the world" or "the moral law" as intelligible independently of linguistic practice.

12. Indeed, disagreement in conclusions is not only possible but common among members of the *same* tradition.

13. See, for example, Henkin, "Religion, Religions, and Human Rights," 231; Perry, *The Idea of Human Rights*, 12–13; and Arvind Sharma, "The Religious Perspective: Dignity as a Foundation for Human Rights Discourse," in *Human Rights and Responsibilities in the World Religions*, ed. Runzo et al., 67–76.

14. Donnelly, "Human Rights and Human Dignity," 312.

15. Adamantia Pollis and Peter Schwab, "Human Rights: A Western Construct with Limited Applicability" in *Human Rights: Cultural and Ideological Perspectives*, ed. Adamantia Pollis and Peter Schwab (New York: Praeger, 1979), 4 and 9.

16. Notice that we claim only that such a conception of human dignity is *necessary*, not that it is *sufficient*. Other ingredients (including structural conditions) also are important to the development of rights thinking. One of these, identified by Annette Baier and noted in chapter 2, is the unwillingness of the weak to beg from the strong.

17. For analogous reasons, as we noted at the end of chapter 2, it does not follow from the fact that the *concept* of human rights is historically contingent (that is, that talk of human rights emerged in a particular historical context) that human rights *themselves* are historically contingent (for example, that prior to the Enlightenment, people did not have human rights) or that they are simply human artifacts.

18. We take it for granted that persuasive means of implementation are to be preferred over coercive ones.

19. It is worth noting, however, that these are not his only objections. He also points out that "every religion at some time, in some respect, has had to answer to the human rights idea for human rights violations, many of them unspeakable" and that religions have often understood morality in terms of *duties*, rather than rights. Henkin, "Religion, Religions, and Human Rights," 229–30 and 232–33.

20. See, for example, John Rawls, *Political Liberalism* (New York: Columbia University Press, 1993), 218.

21. Perry, *The Idea of Human Rights*, 35.

22. Perry canvasses three nonreligious strategies for justifying human rights claims and argues that each is unsuccessful. However, even if Perry is right in each case, the most that his analysis would show is that *these* three nonreligious strategies fail, not that *no* nonreligious strategy could succeed. While we share Perry's skepticism about justifications that aspire to universality in the third sense (as outlined previously), we do not think that it follows that the idea of human rights necessarily requires religious support. In other words, we also want to allow room for nonreligious moral traditions from within which universal human dignity might be affirmed—traditions that are every bit as *particular* as their religious counterparts. (Here it might be helpful to distinguish between nonreligious support and *secular* support, where the latter derives from premises neutral among competing worldviews or conceptions of the good.) Indeed, one strength of the account offered here is that it does not disqualify these nonreligious sources of support, which—because of their particularity—would be ineligible as rational foundations according to Henkin's account.

23. Thus Henkin writes, "If there were a religion that made human rights central, if that religion commanded universal, or nearly universal adherence, such a religion might indeed provide a strong foundation for human rights. But I know of no such religion." Henkin, "Human Rights: Religious or Enlightened?" 34.

24. Of course, to the extent that these declarations carry any moral weight, this will be due to the existence of traditions of moral practice within which such talk can be put into practice—the same traditions within which universal human dignity can be affirmed. As we have argued elsewhere, drawing upon Robert Brandom's work, explicit articulations of moral principles depend upon what is already implicit in

practice. See Amesbury, *Morality and Social Criticism*, chapters 4 and 5. Without the *practice* of human rights, international declarations, however high-minded, remain vacuous and open to abuse and distortion. Given a plurality of moral traditions, some variation of interpretation at the local level is to be expected, even when a particular human rights formulation has been unanimously endorsed, and local insight is to be valued.

25. Henkin, "Religion, Religions, and Human Rights," 239.

26. The problem, to be clear, is not that such endeavors are normative per se, but that they are only covertly, and thus uncritically, so.

27. The term *theology* is of course most appropriate in the context of the various theisms, and particularly within Christianity. In Judaism and Islam, critical religious reflection often takes the form of ethics or legal studies. We thus use the term *theology* only provisionally here.

28. See, for example, Abdullahi A. An-Na'im, "Toward an Islamic Hermeneutics for Human Rights," in *Human Rights and Religious Values: An Uneasy Relationship?* ed. Abdullahi A. An-Na'im et al. (Amsterdam: Editions Rodopi, 1995), 238.

29. He writes, "An 'internal' commitment to a normative regime from one point of view need not and should not be exclusive of the 'other' (however he or she is identified) with respect to a set of commonly agreed human rights. In my view, therefore, what is at issue is not the possibility of abstract or absolute neutrality from any religious, cultural or ideological regime. Rather, the question is how to reconcile commitments to diverse normative regimes with a commitment to a concept and set of universal human rights." Ibid., 229.

30. Significantly, *B'Tselem* is also the name of the Israeli Information Center for Human Rights in the Occupied Territories, an organization dedicated to monitoring and reporting Israeli human rights abuses.

31. Rabbi Gerry Serotta et al., "Rabbinic Letter on Torture," Rabbis for Human Rights–North America, 27 January 2005, http://www.rhr-na.org/initiatives/torture/letter012705B.html (8 June 2006).

32. It is notable that Jewish thinkers and communities have taken a leading role in the campaign to end the genocide in Darfur, Sudan.

33. See, for example, Elliott N. Dorff, "A Jewish Perspective on Human Rights," *Human Rights and Responsibilities in the World Religions*, ed. Runzo et al., 211–13; and Irving

Greenberg, "Grounding Democracy in Reverence for Life: A View from Judaism," in *Religions in Dialogue: From Theocracy to Democracy*, ed. Alan Race and Ingrid Shafer (Aldershot, UK: Ashgate, 2002), 30. For a much more detailed and nuanced study of the relationship between Judaism and human rights, see Peter J. Haas, *Human Rights and the World's Major Religions*, vol. 1, *The Jewish Tradition* (Westport, Conn.: Praeger, 2005).

34. For a survey of this debate, see Robert E. Florida, *Human Rights and the World's Major Religions*, vol. 5, *The Buddhist Tradition* (Westport, Conn.: Praeger, 2005), 9–34.

35. Damien Keown, *Buddhism: A Very Short Introduction* (Oxford: Oxford University Press, 1996), 105. For a fuller development of this argument, see Damien Keown, "Are There 'Human Rights' in Buddhism?" *Journal of Buddhist Ethics* 2 (1995): 3–27.

36. Keith Ward, *Religion and Human Nature* (Oxford: Clarendon, 1998), 324.

37. For a recent example, see the statement "Torture Is a Moral Issue," which was drafted by the National Religious Campaign against Torture and signed by religious leaders from various American traditions, including Christians, Jews, Muslims, and Sikhs. The statement was published as an ad in the *New York Times* on 13 June 2006.

38. It is not necessary to claim that talk of human rights originated exclusively in religion in order to claim a religious *justification* for the idea of human rights. Although its roots are buried in religious soil, the idea of human rights as we know it today emerged in part in reaction to religious abuses. Joseph Heath has remarked that the attempt by religious believers to "take credit" for the idea of human rights is analogous to General Franco trying "to take credit for 'inspiring' Picasso's *Guernica*." Joseph Heath, "Human Rights Have Nothing to Do with Christianity," *Montreal Gazette*, 18 March 2003. However, new ideas typically require justification by reference to what is already accepted, and it is important to distinguish the historical context in which an idea originated from the context(s) in which it can be provided with rational support. It is thus possible for religious believers (of various persuasions) to take *responsibility* for the idea of human rights without taking *credit* for it. Still, as we shall see in the next chapter, some credit is indeed deserved.

5. Christianity and Human Rights: A Historical Perspective

1. Lactantius, *Divinarum Institutionum*, CSEL 19:463–65, PL 6:1061.

2. The medieval background to human rights is usefully examined by Roger Ruston in his *Human Rights and the Image of God* (London: SCM, 2004).

3. Brian Tierney, *Rights, Laws and Infallibility in Medieval Thought* (Aldershot, UK: Variorum, 1997), 174–75.

4. The Reformation brought, of course, a new emphasis on the centrality of scripture. We explore the issue of scriptural interpretation later in the chapter.

5. See Roland Bainton, *The Reformation of the Sixteenth Century* (London: Hodder and Stoughton, 1953); and *Studies on the Reformation* (London: Hodder and Stoughton, 1963).

6. Bainton, *The Reformation of the Sixteenth Century*, 215.

7. Bainton, *Studies on the Reformation*, vii.

8. Of Calvin's authoritarianism, his critic Sebastian Castellio aptly remarked, "To kill a man is not to defend a doctrine. It is to kill a man." Sebastian Castellio, *Contra Libellum Calvini*, Eb, Cal. 77, quoted in Bainton, *The Reformation of the Sixteenth Century*, 177.

9. See Mark A. Noll, *The Civil War as a Theological Crisis* (Chapel Hill, N.C.: University of North Carolina Press, 2006).

10. Daniel Jonah Goldhagen, *Hitler's Willing Executioners: Ordinary Germans and the Holocaust* (New York: Random House, 1996), 110.

11. See John S. Nurser, *For All Peoples and All Nations: The Ecumenical Church and Human Rights* (Washington, D.C.: Georgetown University Press, 2005).

6. Toward a Theology of Human Rights

1. In his homily of November 26, 1978, Oscar Romero said, "The face of Christ is among the sacks and baskets of the farmworker; the face of Christ is among those who are tortured and mistreated in the prisons; the face of Christ is dying of hunger in the children who have nothing to eat." Oscar Romero, quoted in Dennis et al., *Oscar Romero*, 35.

2. Donald W. Shriver Jr., "What Is Forgiveness in a Secular Political Form?" in *Forgiveness and Reconciliation: Religion, Public Policy, and Conflict Transformation*, ed. Raymond G. Helmick and Rodney L. Peterson (Philadelphia: Templeton Foundation, 2001), 162.

3. Desmond Tutu, *No Future without Forgiveness* (New York: Doubleday, 1999), 270.

Index